CAVALRY WIFE
The Diary of
Eveline M. Alexander, 1866–1867

Eveline Martin Alexander and Andrew J. Alexander (*Courtesy George W. Martin*)

CAVALRY WIFE

THE DIARY OF

Eveline M. Alexander, 1866–1867

*Being a Record of Her Journey from New York
to Fort Smith to Join Her Cavalry-Officer Husband,
Andrew J. Alexander, and Her Experiences with Him
on Active Duty Among the Indian Nations and
in Texas, New Mexico, and Colorado*

EDITED WITH AN INTRODUCTION
BY
Sandra L. Myres

Texas A&M University Press

COLLEGE STATION AND LONDON

Library of Congress Cataloging in Publication Data

Alexander, Eveline M. 1843–
  The diary of Eveline M. Alexander, 1866–1867,
being a record of her journey from New York to
Fort Smith to join her cavalry-officer husband,
Andrew J. Alexander, and her experiences with him
on active duty among the Indian nations and in
Texas, New Mexico, and Colorado.

  Bibliography: p.
  Includes index.
  1. Indians of North America—Wars—1865–1895.
2. Alexander, Eveline, 1843–   . 3. Army wives—
United States—Biography. 4. Indians of North
America—Southwest, New—Wars. 5. United States.
Army—Military life. I. Title: The diary of Eveline
M. Alexander, 1866–1867 . . .
E83.866.A43   973.8'1'0924 [B]   76-30611
ISBN 0-89096-025-9

Manufactured in the United States of America
FIRST EDITION

Contents

List of Illustrations

Acknowledgments

AS with any project of this type, the editor is indebted to many people who assisted with the research and preparation of the manuscript. My sincere thanks go to Gerald Pierce for finding the manuscript and providing the opportunity for me to edit it. Many members of Mrs. Alexander's family have gone out of their way to provide assistance. The opportunity to meet and correspond with them has been one of the extraordinary fringe benefits of the editorial work. Mrs. Edward S. (Lois) Blagden and Mr. Robert D. Brewster kindly loaned previously unpublished pictures, and Miss Violet Wilder provided a great deal of helpful information. Mrs. Edward E. (Agnes) Booher supplied not only the letters quoted at the end of the diary but pictures and additional material which enabled me to correct several editorial errors. Very special thanks are due Mrs. Eric (Sylvia) Maude and Mr. George W. Martin for their continuing interest and help. Without their assistance and encouragement the book could never have been completed. Mr. Martin gave me his kind permission to reprint the photographs of Mrs. Alexander, her husband, and other members of her family from *Some Account of Family Stocks Involved in Life at Willowbrook*, by Edward S. Martin.

I am also indebted (as are most historians and authors) to those unsung heroes and heroines of the publishing world— the librarians and archivists. I am especially grateful for the aid and services provided by Mrs. Alma Compton and Mr. J. R. K. Kantor, the Bancroft Library; Miss Barbara Shepherd, Regional History and University Archives, Cornell University; Mr. Elmer Parker, Old Military Records Branch,

National Archives, Washington, D.C.; Mr. C. George Younkin, Archivist, Federal Records Center, Fort Worth, Texas; Mrs. Nancy Wynne and Mrs. Margaret McLean, Amon Carter Museum of Western Art, Fort Worth; Mrs. Nancy Farmer and Mr. Charles Harrell, University of Texas at Arlington; and particularly Mr. Stephen C. Erskine, the Seymour Library, Auburn, New York.

My thanks also go to my colleagues who offered assistance and encouragement: Dr. Martin Hall, Department of History; Dr. Stanton Garner, Department of English; and Mr. John Hudson, Librarian, University of Texas at Arlington. I also appreciate the assistance of Mr. James Wilson, Museum of New Mexico, Santa Fe; Dr. Ron Tyler, Amon Carter Museum; and especially Miss Francine Morris, University of Texas at Arlington, who has been my chief proofreader, critic, and "girl Friday."

The Bancroft Library, Mrs. Sylvia Maude, Mrs. Phyllis B. Mitchell, and Mr. Robert D. Brewster kindly provided the necessary permissions to publish the manuscript. Funds for the research and travel involved in preparing the diary for publication were provided through a grant from the Liberal Arts Organized Research Fund, University of Texas at Arlington.

Finally, my sincere appreciation goes to Evy Alexander, whose charm, wit, and adventurous spirit are reflected in her journal. I have tried to determine what changes and editorial comments she would have made had she prepared the diary for publication. I hope that I have succeeded in doing her justice.

Introduction

AMONG the most popular and informative descriptions of life in the nineteenth-century American West are the numerous accounts written by the officers and men of the United States Army. These range from official journals of expeditions and campaigns and formal histories of various units to diaries, books, and personal memoirs published by generals, captains, lieutenants, and even an occasional enlisted man. Some of the army authors, like Generals Sherman, Sheridan, and Crook, were concerned with strategy and planning on a broad scale or with justifying their own programs and plans, while others, like Captain Carter, Lieutenant Sweeny, and Trooper Lowe, were content to recount the history and campaigns of one or two units or to recall details of life at a single post. Although uneven in quality and information, all these narratives give an added dimension and a deeper perception to our view of western military life, and the better ones—such as Captain John G. Bourke's *On the Border with Crook*—are found in almost every western bibliography and are considered required reading for anyone interested in the American West.[1]

The Ladies—Bless 'Em

Ranking along with their husbands as chroniclers of life in the West are the army wives whose articles and books historian Robert M. Utley has correctly labeled minor frontier classics.[2] Far from home, confined to often inadequate and uncomfortable quarters in what seemed to most of them a barren, inhospitable land totally different from anything they had known in the moist, green eastern valleys, the ladies present a picture of western life very different from that of their husbands. The wives are understandably more concerned with the difficulties of making a home and raising a family than they are with military strategy or campaigns against hostile Indians. Their narratives tend to concentrate on events of home and garrison life, or, as Elizabeth Custer phrased it, "the domestic life of an army family . . . our occupations, amusements, and mode of housekeeping . . . and in some instances . . . the trifling perplexities and events which went to fill up the sum of our existence."[3]

Although many of the army wives kept diaries, journals, or notes on their experiences, most of those writings were never intended for publication. The ladies wrote out of boredom, frustration, loneliness, and occasionally fear, confiding to paper the thoughts and impressions they would not or could not mention to their often overworked and certainly underpaid husbands. Some of the women later prepared their reminiscences for their children or grandchildren or published stories of their army life in order to supplement small pensions, but most of their narratives were lost or forgotten. A few found their way into archival collections, where from time to time they have come to light. Such is the case of the account written by Eveline (or Evelina)[4] Throop Martin Alexander, whose letters and journal, kept as a weekly report for her parents, are herein published for the first time. Mrs. Alexander thus joins a distinguished group of women, including Elizabeth Custer, Lydia Spencer Lane, Teresa Viélé, Ellen McGowen Biddle, and Martha Summerhayes, whose recollections of army life in the West have added greatly to our knowledge and understanding of the nineteenth-century frontier.[5]

Eveline Alexander

Eveline was born February 28, 1843, in Utica, New York, the fourth child of Enos Throop Thompson Martin and Cornelia Williams. Evy's father was the nephew of Enos Thompson Throop, a prominent Jacksonian Democrat and governor of New York from 1829 to 1833. During his uncle's first term, Martin served as the governor's private secretary and aide. Following this apprenticeship in politics, Martin "read law," probably in the Auburn, New York, offices of William Seward, and then entered a New York firm headed by John Lorimer Graham. In 1837 Martin married Cornelia Williams, an attractive young heiress whose father, John Williams, had large investments in railroads, packet boats, mills, and mercantile establishments. The young Martins made their home in New York City for several years, enjoying the social and business life of the city. Their first three children, Mary Williams, usually called Molly; Cornelia Eliza, known as Nelly; and Harriet Byron, who died in infancy, were born there.

About 1844, Martin purchased his Uncle Throop's farm, Willowbrook, on Lake Owasco just outside Auburn, and the family moved to the more congenial rural atmosphere. Four other children, John Williams (Jack), George Bliss, Edward Sanford (Ned), and Violet Blair, were born at the Auburn farm.

The Martins were in what was often described in the nineteenth century as "comfortable circumstances," and Martin could well afford to lead the life of a gentleman farmer. Soon after moving to Willowbrook he gave up his law practice and devoted himself to a careful management of his properties, his wife's fortune, and his collection of fine and rare books. As one of his children recalled, Martin "was a careful man, very devoted to his family, highly responsible, amusing but far from frivolous, and with a natural gift not only of humor but of authority."[6] His children were fond of him despite his occasional authoritarian pronouncements, and his literary tastes obviously influenced his children. All were enthusiastic readers, as evidenced by Evy's large "traveling library" and frequent references throughout her journal to books she was reading. Martin also wrote occasional articles and reviews and for many years published a regular column in the *New York Knickerbocker*. He evidently encouraged other members of the family to share his avocation. Mrs. Martin contributed to missionary magazines and historical journals and eventually published a book of reminiscences entitled *The Old Home*. Edward became one of the founding editors of the *Harvard Lampoon* and later achieved a national reputation as an editor and publisher.[7] Evy also contributed to an occasional missionary tract and wrote a few pieces for local newspapers. She may have intended to publish her western journal. Certainly her father was instrumental in her decision to keep such a record, and he may well have had in mind an eventual book or series of articles.

The household at Willowbrook was a large and active one. In addition to the eleven Martin children, their tutors and governesses, and several relatives, including former Governor Throop, there were many houseguests. The family was well acquainted with a number of people through their political and social associations, and Willowbrook often played host to visiting dignitaries. Ambassadors, cabinet officers, senators, authors, journalists, and well-known businessmen were frequent guests, and Evy and her brothers and sisters grew up in an atmosphere which brought them into contact with many of the famous men and women of the day. Thus, it is not surprising that Evy does not seem particularly awed by the prospect of entertaining General Sherman in her tent home at Spanish Peaks, or that she finds the social life of the army somewhat dull in comparison to her home experiences.

Among the Martins' closest friends were Francis Preston Blair, Sr., editor of the *Washington Globe*, and his wife, Eliza Violet. The Blair children often spent the summer at Willowbrook while the Martin girls visited Silver Springs and were introduced to Washington society under the Blairs' sponsorship. It was through this close family friendship that Evy met her future husband, Andrew Jonathan Alexander.

Alexander (born in 1833) was the youngest son of Andrew J. Alexander of Sherwood, Kentucky, and Mira Madison, the daughter of Major George Madison of Frankfort, Kentucky. Like Evy, Andrew was educated at home by a succession of tutors. He later attended college at Danville, Kentucky. When the Civil War began, Alexander was preparing to go into business in Saint Louis. Instead, he joined the Union

Army as lieutenant in the First Regiment of Mounted Rifles (later the Third Cavalry) and was sent east for duty on Mc-Clellan's staff. Alexander was related to a number of prominent families, including the Biddles, Madisons, Prestons, and Blairs, and during his Washington service he was frequently a guest at the Blairs' Silver Springs home. Undoubtedly it was during one of her visits to Silver Springs that Evy met the dashing young cavalry officer described by his friend, Major General James B. Wilson, as standing over six feet tall, with "a superb figure . . . stately carriage, bright flashing blue eyes . . . flowing beard, as tawny as a lion's mane . . . and hair that glistened like gold in the sunshine. . . ."[8] However much Wilson's flowery prose may have overstated the case, Alexander was evidently a handsome and personable young man. Eveline, attractive, well educated, and a close friend of Alexander's cousins, the Blairs, seemed a perfect match. On November 3, 1864, the two were married in the Sand Beach church near Willowbrook.

The bridegroom soon returned to duty and served until the end of the war with the Division of the Mississippi, partic-ipating in the final campaigns in Tennessee, Alabama, and Georgia. By the end of the war, Alexander held the rank of brevet colonel in the regular army and had been recommended for a brevet brigadier generalship in recognition of his "dis-tinguished skill and gallantry in the cavalry engagements at Ebenezer Church and Columbus, Georgia."[9] On several oc-casions he had been singled out by his superiors for commenda-tion, and he had a number of friends and admirers in the army high command. He therefore decided to remain in the army instead of returning to an uncertain business career. In July, 1865, Alexander accepted an assignment as inspector general and chief of staff to his former commander, General George Stoneman, who was stationed in eastern Tennessee. Eveline soon joined her husband at Knoxville and thus began a twenty-year period of army service. According to Eveline, army life was in most ways very satisfactory: "In our pro-fession we are spared all the annoyances of insurance, taxes, & etc. . . . and we have only one thing to take care of—to see that our expenses do not exceed our income. . . . Andrew and

I very often discuss the pros and cons of army life and we always come to the conclusion that take it all together it is a good place."[10]

In 1866 Alexander was ordered to New Mexico for duty with the Third Cavalry, and it was in conjunction with this phase of their army service that Eveline began her journal. "I keep a daily journal," she wrote her mother during the first weeks of the trip, "and whenever I have the opportunity I copy a few pages, so that I may have the duplicate ready to send you when I get to Fort Union."[11]

As revealed in her journal, Evy "took kindly" to camp life. She was young, healthy, exuberant, and without numerous responsibilities, and thus was able to enjoy the journey. To this extent she was somewhat unusual among the army wives, for, with the exception of Elizabeth Custer, few of them relished the long overland trips to western duty stations. For the young Alexanders, however, the trip was something of a second honeymoon, and they took advantage of the time to ride, hunt, and enjoy the beauty of the western country. Evy also enjoyed their year in New Mexico. "To hear many of the officers' wives here talk you would think New Mexico was a purgatory, and their husbands are no better," she wrote her mother. "On the contrary I have enjoyed myself exceedingly here, and have never had a sad hour. . . ."[12]

In 1867 the Alexanders left New Mexico and, after a short visit to Willowbrook, proceeded to Washington, where Andrew reported to President Grant on his inspection of the New Mexico posts. By January, 1868, the Alexanders were again on their way west, this time to the newly established Fort McDowell, Arizona, where Andrew served as commanding officer and military supervisor for the Verde district.[13] The Alexanders' first child, a daughter, was born at McDowell in September, 1868. The following year the family moved to Camp Hualapai near Prescott, where Alexander assumed command of the post and continued his duties as district supervisor. In 1870 Alexander received an extended leave and took Eveline and baby Midge home to Willowbrook. For the next

four years Andrew alternated between service in the West—
where he headed the garrisons at Fort Bayard, New Mexico,
and Fort Garland, Colorado—and duty in New York and
Washington as a member of a special board convened to revise
army regulations. In late 1874 the Alexanders returned to Fort
Union, New Mexico, where Andrew served as post commander.

Up to this time the Alexanders had had a happy and
successful life. Eveline's good humor and satisfaction with
their sometimes onerous assignments was probably based as
much on their good fortune and generally pleasant experiences as on her love for the West. Shortly after their return
to New Mexico, however, their lives were changed by a series
of family tragedies. Evy's sister, Emily Upton, and her be-
loved uncle, former governor Throop, died, and a few years
later the Alexanders were saddened by the loss of their close
friends Myles Keogh (at the Little Big Horn) and Emily's
husband, Emory Upton (by suicide). Even more tragic for the
Alexanders was the loss of their young daughter, Midge, who
died of an undiagnosed illness just a few weeks after their
arrival at Fort Union. Although Eveline gave birth to a son
the following year, neither Evy nor Andrew ever recovered
from their daughter's death.

Between 1875 and 1879 the Alexanders were in Texas,
where Andrew commanded the garrisons at Fort Brown and
Ringgold Barracks. From 1879 to 1881 Andrew served with
the Second Cavalry at Fort Ellis and Fort Custer, Montana.
However, the long years of frontier service had taken their
toll. Shortly after the Alexanders' arrival at Fort Custer,
Andrew became seriously ill and returned east on sick leave.
His health gradually improved, but he was unable to rejoin
his regiment. He retired from the army in 1885 and died a
year later.[14]

Eveline, left with a young son and a small pension, returned to Willowbrook, where she lived until her death in
1922. For several years Evy and her unmarried sister, Nelly,
supplemented their income by operating a successful canning
and baking business. In later years George Martin and the

Tremain and Wilder families joined the household, creating a "Willowbrook Compound" not unlike the famous twentieth-century complex at Hyannisport, Massachusetts.

The last years of her life understandably affected Eveline's personality. The cheerful, optimistic, occasionally impulsive girl of the journal disappeared, replaced by a commanding yet gentle woman of great strength and serious demeanor. Although greatly respected and loved by her many nieces and nephews, Eveline's final years were filled with yearning for her husband and children (her only surviving child, Upton, died in 1910). Many of the present generation recall "Aunt Evy" with great affection, but most would agree that the "Great Matriarch of the Upper House," as one nephew termed her, was very different from the Eveline who wrote the diary.[15]

The Diary

Although a number of reminiscences by army wives have been published and several have been reissued in new editions, many others written during the late nineteenth century remain undiscovered in trunks, family papers, and regional archives. Eveline Alexander's journal would have shared such a fate except for a happy set of circumstances. In the spring of 1970, Dr. Gerald Pierce of Memphis State University discovered Eveline Alexander's diary in the extensive manuscript collections of the Bancroft Library of the University of California at Berkeley. Dr. Pierce asked me to examine the text with a view toward editing and annotating it. The Bancroft Library kindly provided a microfilm copy, I read it, and I found myself delighted with Evy's descriptions, narrative, and refreshing naiveté and *joie de vivre*. I immediately set about the task of checking provenance, verifying the manuscript, and securing the necessary permissions for publication. Unfortunately, the Bancroft Library did not hold literary rights and had very little information on the origin of the journal, which had become part of their collections long before anyone concerned themselves with formalities of provenance.

Several months of searching for information on Eveline's heirs proved fruitless until Mr. Stephen Erskine of the Seymour Library in Auburn, New York, quite above and beyond the call of duty, personally undertook the task of searching out heirs through wills, deeds, and bills of sale for the Willowbrook property. Through the hard work and good offices of Mr. Erskine, I was able to contact Eveline's literary heirs and other members of the family. All were most gracious and courteous, but they had little information on the diary. Although Eveline had mentioned her "weekly journal" in some of her letters, no one in the immediate family had seen the manuscript, nor were they aware that there was an extant copy.

Finally, Mr. George Martin of New York provided the key. He recalled that, according to his father, "Aunt Evy" had sent part of her journal to her brother-in-law, General Emory Upton, when Upton was stationed at Presidio San Francisco.[16] Probably, then, the journal was among Upton's effects at the time of his death and eventually went to the Bancroft Library. So far as I have been able to discover, the Bancroft manuscript is the only surviving portion of the diary. From all external and internal evidence it is authentic, and I have accepted George Martin's theory of its probable provenance.

Although many of the army wives kept some sort of diary, Eveline Alexander's is the first to be published in its original form. It thus avoids a criticism sometimes leveled at other reminiscences, since Eveline did not have an opportunity to edit the manuscript or change her original impressions and ideas. This lends her work an authenticity sometimes lacking in the writings of the other army wives. The fact that this is a journal written partly as a weekly report to her parents gives it a conversational instead of a literary tone. The same spontaneity is evident in Eveline's letters, in her reports of life on the plains, and in the good humor and obvious delight with which she greeted new experiences. Elizabeth Custer has something of the same approach to her subject despite the more serious purpose of her books in protecting and enhancing her husband's reputation. As Jane Stewart points out in her introduction to a recent edition of Mrs. Custer's *Following the Guidon,* "[Mrs. Custer's] books were not written in the high-toned literary style quite common to literary ladies of that period, but rather as if she were carrying on a conversation with friends."[17] Much the same comment might be made about Eveline Alexander's work.

When reading Eveline's diary, one is reminded of the charming journal of Susan Shelby Magoffin, who, although not an army wife, did travel the Santa Fe Trail before the Mexican War. Mrs. Magoffin's circumstances were somewhat different from those encountered by Mrs. Alexander, but Susan's carefree and happy approach to western travel is similar to Eveline's. Both young women share an enthusiasm for the western landscape and a sense of adventure and exuberant spirit.

Despite her Victorian values, Eveline was able to react with ease and good humor to the conditions imposed by the trail and frontier society. While in the West, she remained strong on temperance and church attendance, but she moderated her previously held views on race. Her attitudes toward frontier conditions and culture are much less critical than those of most of the army wives, and she adapted to her surroundings rather than attempting to change the West to conform with eastern standards of comfort and propriety. Eveline is also different from most of her sisters-in-arms in her attitudes to both American Indians and blacks. Her religious background and missionary zeal led her to interest herself more than the other women in the problems of the Indians, particularly the Navajos, and her views, interpretations, and misinterpretations of native American life on the plains and in New Mexico are much more detailed than those of most other army wives who wrote about the same time. Moreover, to the best of my knowledge, Eveline is the only army wife who wrote fairly extensively about Negro troops. Today her views seem narrow, even racist, but they do give a perspective on the problems faced by black soldiers in the years immediately following the Civil War which is difficult to find in similar source materials.

Eveline did not take part in any great historical events or major military campaigns, but her diary does offer interesting new views of several sidelights of western history. Her reports on the mutiny of the Fifty-seventh Infantry at Fort Smith and her descriptions of Fort Stevens during its brief existence supplement very meager sources on these two events, while her recollections of Sherman and Carson bring new insights into the characters of these historically important men.

A Word on Methodology

In choosing an editorial method for Eveline's diary, I found myself in something of a dilemma. I wanted to retain as much of the original form as possible, but at the same time I wished to prepare an easily readable narrative. Unlike a manuscript by a well-known or important author, the diary of a relatively obscure army wife had no particular literary interest in and of itself. No one reading Eveline Alexander's journal is likely to care how she spells Canadian River or where or how she places her punctuation, and I seriously doubt that scholars, literary or historical, will prepare critical comments on her use of language. The diary is typical in writing style of those kept by many women during the late nineteenth century, and Evy will be read, if she is read at all, for her narrative, not her literary merit. Thus, in editing her diary I have tried to make the text readable by regularizing grammar. At the same time, I have attempted to preserve the diarist's style and individuality. This has occasioned several editorial liberties for which I beg the scholar's pardon but which I trust will make the diary more enjoyable. For those who wish to consult it, the original manuscript is available in the Bancroft Library, and it can be obtained in both microfilm and copyflow.

There are a number of errors in spelling and punctuation in the diary, but considering the difficulties under which Eveline wrote, it is surprising that there are not more. One can

picture her jotting down a quick impression as her ambulance
bounces along the Whipple route or over the Raton Pass or
imagine her bending over her journal after the evening meal,
the inevitable "pups" chasing back and forth, a lantern or
candle flickering on a nearby camp table, as she tries to recall
the events of the day or figure out a phonetic spelling for some
strange new word or incomprehensible place name.

In general I have regularized Eveline's spelling, capitali-
zation, and punctuation and have spelled out her abbreviations.
I have also corrected obvious "slips of the pen"—costome for
costume, an occasionally repeated word, and the like—but I
have retained her rather unusual spellings of French, Spanish,
and Indian words and phrases. In an additional attempt to
prevent unnecessary breaks in the text, I have used only spar-
ingly the scholarly notation *sic*. The diary has been edited
without deletions from the original text. Where necessary for
clarity or smoothness, a few words have been added. These are
enclosed in brackets, which I trust will not be overly disrup-
tive.

I have taken considerable editorial liberty with punctuation. One must remember that Eveline was keeping a journal,
not writing for publication, and she frequently used dashes to
tie together long sentences and inserted numerous commas as
if she had paused in her writing and decided to throw in a
comma while she mulled things over. Her other punctuation is
also irregular and inconsistent. Thus, while attempting to preserve the flavor of the original, I have made numerous changes
and in a few places have recast her sentences as a general aid
to the reader. I suspect that Eveline would have made such
corrections herself if she had prepared the journal for publication.

The chapter breaks are artificial ones provided both for
design purposes and as a convenience to the reader. We have
become so accustomed to this device that it is often disconcert-
ing if it is not used. The subheadings in the table of contents
are, in the same way, an editorial device intended to impart the
style and feeling of many published nineteenth-century works
of this type. As explained in the text, the last part of the jour-

nal is missing. In order to round out the narrative, and with the kind permission of Mrs. Edward Booher, I have quoted from Eveline's letters for the last few months of the Alexanders' stay in New Mexico. Perhaps other portions of the diary for the 1867–1868 period may someday come to light.

SANDRA L. MYRES

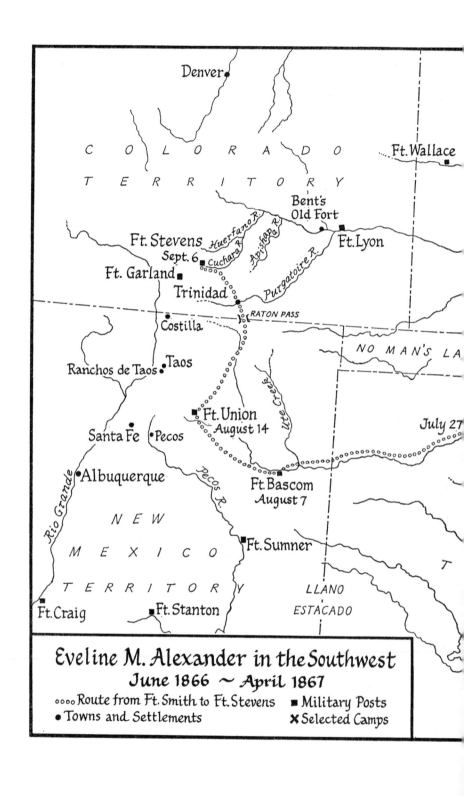

Denver•

C O L O R A D O

T E R R I T O R Y

Ft.Wallace

Bent's
Old Fort

Ft.Stevens *Huerfano R.*
Sept. 6 *Cuchara* *Apishapa R.* Ft.Lyon
Ft. Garland■
Trinidad *Purgatoire R.*
RATON PASS

Costilla•

NO MAN'S LA

•Taos
Ranchos de Taos•

Ute Creek

July 27

■Ft.Union
August 14

Santa Fe• •Pecos

•Albuquerque

Pecos R.

Ft.Bascom
August 7

N E W

Rio Grande

M E X I C O

■Ft. Sumner

T E R R I T O R Y

LLANO
ESTACADO

T

Ft.Craig■ ■Ft.Stanton

Eveline M. Alexander in the Southwest
June 1866 ~ April 1867
∘∘∘∘ Route from Ft. Smith to Ft.Stevens ■ Military Posts
• Towns and Settlements ✗ Selected Camps

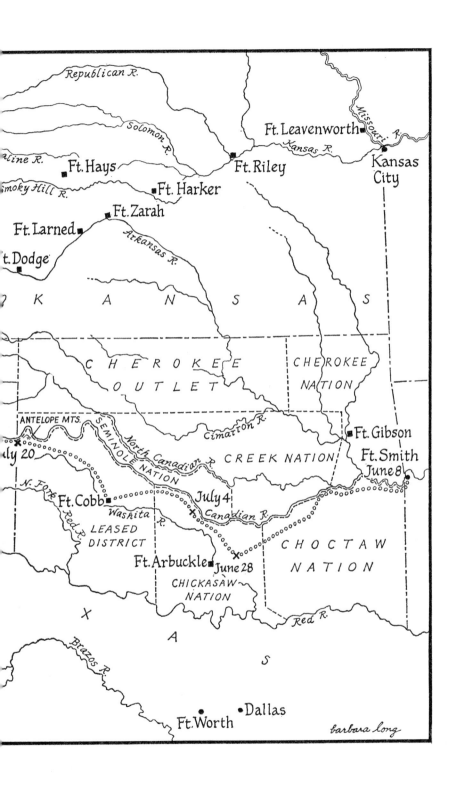

Republican R.

Solomon R.

aline R.

Smoky Hill R.

Ft. Hays

Ft. Harker

Ft. Zarah

Ft. Larned

t. Dodge

Arkansas R.

Ft. Leavenworth

Kansas R.

Ft. Riley

Missouri R.

Kansas City

A R K A N S A S

C H E R O K E E

O U T L E T

CHEROKEE NATION

ANTELOPE MTS.

ly 20

SEMINOLE NATION

North Canadian R.

Cimarron R.

CREEK NATION

Ft. Gibson

Ft. Smith
June 8

N. Fork

Ft. Cobb

July 4

Canadian R.

Washita R.

Red R.

LEASED
DISTRICT

Ft. Arbuckle
June 28

CHICKASAW
NATION

C H O C T A W

N A T I O N

X

A

Red R.

Brazos R.

S

Ft. Worth

Dallas

barbara long

CAVALRY WIFE
The Diary of
Eveline M. Alexander, 1866–1867

I

A Long Journey Begins

New York to Arkansas, May–June, 1866

April 30, 1866
Willowbrook[1]

Day before yesterday I received a telegram from my husband from Little Rock telling me to join him. So I expect to start this week for Arkansas. I feel distressed today. "I am in a strait betwixt two, having a desire to depart." When I think of Andrew I am happy, but when I think of leaving my father, my mother, my home people, I feel a sinking of heart. I am going so far away and for such an indefinite time that it seems like the first parting from home. I almost wish I was not going. And yet Andrew is so lonely.

Today I bade goodbye to my Sunday school class. There were eleven there. Newton Adriance, George DeGroff, Frank Perry, John Van Arsdale, John Adriance, William Bauer, George and Ned, Alfred Williamson, John Chamberlain, Oscar Casey.[2] I told them that I was to leave them and gave them my parting advice. We all agreed to pray for each other Saturday evening at sunset. I promised to write them from New Mexico. I talked to Newton Adriance and George DeGroff afterwards and committed the class to their immediate care. I feel a deep interest in this class which I have had so long. Oh, that they may all be brought into the fold. I used to always say I was raising these boys to be elders and deacons.

Oh, my heart fails me so when I think of leaving my father. What should I do if I should never see him again? But I will remember God's kindness to me in the past and find my strength in Him. All of this family are so dear to me. It will be an agony to leave any one of them. I see my father's heart is heavy at the thought of my going.

May 3

This last week has been a week of changes. I have heard by telegraph from [General] Comstock several times of officers who are going to the Third [Cavalry], but their plans have all been altered.[3] Last night we got another telegram from Andrew. It said, "When did my wife leave? I leave next week." Upon this I came to the conclusion to start the next night alone. I slept with mother, [and] we both passed rather an agitated night. Mother sent a telegram to father at Utica early in the morning, stating the case and saying I started that night. He replied he would be home in the afternoon to go with me. The best of fathers—the most self-sacrificing of mothers.

The day was spent in the toil of packing. Father arrived at noon, and in the evening we left for Rochester. It was very hard parting from my mother and family. We went together into her library and there united in prayer for each other and for every one of the family. I could not prevent the sad thought from entering my mind that perhaps our farewell was for ever. My mother is so very delicate.[4] But we both agreed that we would trust in Him who has been our keeper thus far and who has never suffered the evil we have sometimes anticipated to come to us. Uncle felt my going keenly. When he embraced me, he said, "I may be here when you return, but it is hardly probable."[5] Dear Jack's eyes were filled with tears when he kissed me. Ah me! It was a sad thing all around, and I had to whisper continually to myself "Andrew! Andrew!" that I might get strength to go. The torturing thought would come to me, "Shall I be back and will they *all* be here when I come?"

Father and I had a long talk together on the cars that evening about the family. He takes a great deal of comfort with his boys.

May 5
Cincinnati, Ohio

We have gotten thus far on our journey, and when I opened my eyes in the sleeping car this morning, I found full leafed summer had come upon us. I spent the day with father's new friends, the Andersons, and was very much pleased with them. Mrs. Anderson has a family of ten boys—what a household. They are all very much interested in Henry Bradford's engagement to a friend and neighbor of theirs, Lizzie Phipps, and agree with father in thinking that he should defer his journey till after his marriage. I left word for him that I believed that I should see the Rocky Mountains before he did.

Left Cincinnati this evening for Saint Louis.

May 6
Odin, Illinois

I am spending Sunday in one of these mushroom western towns. Father and I met a gentleman from Texas, an ex-rebel officer, on the train last night, and from what he told us we came to the conclusion that I could save about two days by going direct to Cairo. So, as I think there is little probability of Frank and Apo being in Saint Louis,[6] I have concluded to take this route.

This is rather a heathenish place; none of the servants at the tavern knew where a church was. However, I discovered one at last and attended it. It was a square brick building—two storied. In the upper part was held the "Church of the Disciples," as I was told. The ground floor was devoted to the Presbyterians. We had a curious sermon full of western expressions—the shorter catechism was "as full of bible truths as an egg is of meat." I found a class without a teacher at the Sunday school before church and sowed a little seed by the wayside.[7]

May 7
On board Steamer *Magenta*, Mississippi River

We arrived in Cairo this morning just in time to catch the boat. Father got me a stateroom and had me comfortably fixed when the steamer whistled, and he had just time to kiss me and say, "Goodbye my darling. God bless you and keep you." and he was gone. My heart sank within me when he left me. It may be for years, and I am still so far away from Andrew.

I went out on deck as the boat moved off and watched the

meeting of the waters of the Ohio and Mississippi. For some distance after they flowed together the two rivers were easily distinguishable by their color. I spent most of the day up in the pilothouse, where I had a full view of the "mighty Mississippi." The river is grand from its breadth and volume of water, but it is not a beautiful river: the water is excessively muddy, and the shores are not picturesque. I am told above Saint Louis the scenery is very fine, and below Napoleon it is interesting on account of the fine cotton plantations that border it on either side.

The gentleman I am with, Mr. Thomas B. Lincoln of Texas,[8] interests me very much. He tells me a great deal of his life and of his experiences while in the Rebel army.

May 8

I was very much amused this morning to discover that on retiring last night, while I took the extraordinary precaution of loading my little pistol and putting it under my pillow, I had neglected the very ordinary precaution of locking my door.

We reached Memphis about 7 A.M. General Stoneman met me on the boat and gave me a hearty welcome. A boat bound for White River was lying at the levee, so I had my baggage carried on board at once. General Stoneman took me home with him, where I found Mrs. Stoneman and her sister Alice. I remained until 5 P.M. and had a very pleasant visit with them. Mrs. Stoneman grieves very much for her mother. She seemed sad and not in good health. They were very kind and affectionate to me. General Stoneman took me to the boat and saw me off and said to me, "It is almost like parting with a sister to say goodbye to you."[9]

May 10
White River Steamer *Commercial*

This is the second day of my voyage up this strange-looking river. So far I have seen only one spot of terra firma, and I hear it is all I shall see till I reach DeVall's Bluff.[10] The country on either side is flooded over from five to forty miles. The river is narrow and deep, and one can readily imagine

Eveline's father and mother, Enos Thompson Throop Martin and Cornelia
Williams Martin (*Courtesy George W. Martin*)

Eveline's sisters Nelly (above) and Molly (*Courtesy George W. Martin*)

Eveline's sister Emily and her husband, Emory Upton (*Courtesy George W. Martin*)

Eveline's sister Lylie and her husband, Grenville Tremain (*Courtesy George W. Martin*)

Eveline's brother Throop Martin and youngest sister, Violet (*Courtesy George W. Martin*)

Myles Keogh (left) and Andrew Alexander (*Courtesy Robert D. Brew-ster*)

Emily, Nelly, Lylie, and Myles Keogh (*Courtesy George W. Martin*)

The Upper House at Willowbrook. Eveline stands fourth from the right, Andrew second from the right, and Enos Martin third from the left. Mrs. Martin is seated in the center; the white-haired man on the far right of the group is Eveline's great-uncle Enos Thompson Throop. The others are members of the immediate Martin family. (*Courtesy Lois Martin Blagden*)

one's self sailing through one of those strange submerged forests in South America instead of winding through the swamps of Arkansas.

I have picked up another rebel as a *compagnion de voyage* —a Major Busbie of Arkansas. He has been very attentive and quite communicative concerning "the Madam and the little fellows" who live in Pine's Bluff on the Arkansas. I have gotten quite well acquainted with all in the ladies' cabin. I have been most interested in a Tennessee lady who married and lives in Pennsylvania. Her husband is here with her. We have talked together for two days, and tonight, by the merest accident, I discovered they were from Reading and that her husband is Harry Keim's brother. Of course we immediately became great friends when we made this discovery.

I saw something of life such as I have read of on one of these southern streamers. In the evening I was most urgently requested to "take a hand in a little game of cards," the gentlemen reassuring me by saying they never bet more than so much on a game. There was also a gay dance in the cabin in which I was invited to participate but declined.

May 11

This morning about 6 A.M. arrived at DeVall's Bluff, and never had I seen a spot which seemed so entirely the "jumping off place" as this. Here I was met by Sergeant McMasters of G Company with a note from Andrew telling me he was on his way to Fort Smith, where he would "await me with open arms," etc. Of course I was disappointed enough that I should not meet my husband at Little Rock as I had hoped. I was attended to at "the Bluff" by some acquaintance of Andrew's who was very polite. Here I first came in contact with officers of Negro troops, and I was shocked to find them more low and uneducated than I had supposed them.

Left DeVall's Bluff at noon and arrived at Little Rock about five in the midst of a terrific thunder and hail storm. Major Rawles met me at the cars and took me [to his] home, where I received a warm welcome from Fanny.

Andrew left several days ago, and I have concluded to remain here awhile so as to give Andrew abundant time to get to Fort Smith before I join him.

May 15

Arkansas River, Steamer *I. Hall*

Left Little Rock this afternoon. I have had a charming visit here. Fanny and her husband were most devoted in their attentions. Colonel Floyd Jones of the Nineteenth [Infantry] has been exceedingly polite. He was down on the boat to see me off today. Last night I had a charming serenade from the band of the Nineteenth. Colonel and Mrs. Moale are also here.

May 18

Fort Smith, Arkansas

I arrived here this morning after a tiresome trip from "the Rock." The weather was hot and the steamer very slow, and it seemed as if we would never get here. The shores of the Arkansas are very picturesque, but I cared for nothing but the sight of Fort Smith. We got here about five this morning, and before long I was in my husband's arms. He was very glad to see me and felt like I did when he came to me at Washington that we must "never part again."

My ambulance was waiting for me,[11] and soon we were at "Camp Reynolds" about two miles from the fort. The first thing that greeted my eyes was Fan and five of her litter of twelve pups, and it was about as pretty a sight as I ever saw. A litter of pointer pups—pureblood and beautifully marked. The finest of all is called Jack, and Andrew is going to train him for his namesake.[12]

May 22

I have been several days in camp now and take to it very kindly. I have everything arranged most comfortably for me. My tent is lined with blue army blankets, which not only protect it from dampness and make it much cooler on hot days, but subdue the light, which makes a distressing glare in the canvas tents. I have a buffalo skin for a carpet, and my bed is covered with the red blanket Fanny Rawles gave me.

Today we had a review of the regiment, which was very

interesting. Colonel Howe insisted I should ride by his side during the review and wanted me to receive the salute as reviewing officer, but the last compliment I declined. I rode Zaidee (the first time since Knoxville) and wore my grey riding habit and black velvet hat. Zaidee behaved beautifully. After the regiment had passed in review before the colonel, we rode along the line and, as the ground was rough and full of ditches, Zay distinguished herself. The first ditch we came to was rather wide, but she took it like a bird and behaved throughout with the most perfect decorum. Zaidee was very much complimented on her behavior and appearance.

May 23

This morning we were to have started on our journey across the plains. The Negro regiment, the Fifty-seventh U.S. Colored,[13] which was to act as pioneers, were ordered to march when [their] colonel came and reported to Colonel Howe that it had mutinied and refused to go. The Third [Cavalry] was ordered out under arms and was soon there. The darkies were excessively frightened when they saw themselves surrounded and threw down their arms, professing their willingness to go "anywhere, anywhere with the colonel."[14]

Colonel Howe behaved exceedingly well, or, as the officers say, "like a trump" throughout the affair. He is not at all a popular man. However, he is very kind to me and very complimentary to Andrew.

I went in today and called on Mrs. Barnard of the Nineteenth Infantry and Mrs. Captain Churchill. They have been very attentive since I came.

May 26

A "rainy day in camp." I find it much more endurable than I would have imagined. Andrew had a camp kettle full of coals brought up from the company kitchen and put in the door of my tent, and this made me very comfortable. The only thing that disturbs me in camp is the frightful profanity. It is not quite so bad now as when we first came. I heard Andrew threatening the buglers who stand at the back of our tent this morning that he would "cut them over the head with the sabre" if he caught them swearing around his quarters, in token of which, I suppose, his sabre was hanging at the door of the tent.

May 29

George's birthday. He is twelve years old today and promoted to the use of a gun, I believe. I would have written him, but I sent him a letter a few days ago giving an account of the "pups." I wrote to Molly on the fourteenth.[15]

The "womenkind" in this regiment are rather a queer set. Mrs. C. was a company washwoman before her husband was promoted from the ranks. Mrs. K. and her daughter are very common. Mrs. H. and "Patrita" are Mexicans. I have not seen them. Besides this there is Mrs. Sutorius, a bride of nineteen from New York, not highly educated, but well-behaved, and I like her. Another bride makes up our number, a child of fourteen that Lieutenant Carroll married just before leaving Little Rock. She seems an innocent little girl, ignorant alike of good or of evil, perfectly uneducated, but I am interested in her and would gladly do anything for her.

June 7

Andrew got a letter from Colonel Floyd Jones this morning. It came with the returned mutineers who have been sent back from Little Rock to accompany us—*nolens, volens*! We are very much disgusted at the prospect of taking them with us. There is a great deal of ill feeling between the two regiments.

Colonel Jones tells us that General Scott is dead. He also says that Keogh had been appointed to the Fourth Cavalry.[16] I am glad he has received an appointment, but am very sorry it is in the Fourth, which is noted among cavalry regiments for hard drinking.

I like Colonel Jones very much, and I was rather prejudiced against him before I met him at Little Rock. He is very gentlemanly and has been exceedingly courteous to me.

Andrew and I dined today at the garrison with Mrs. Barnard. She is a very pleasant woman, and so is Mrs. Churchill.

II

Indian Territory

Fort Smith to Fort Cobb, June–July, 1866

June 8

Yesterday the first column, under charge of Captain How-land, left Camp Reynolds. This morning the second column under Colonel Alexander, consisting of companies A (Hawley and McMullen), D (Cain), G (Alexander and Mulford), and I (Tarleton and Russel), were ordered to march. The colonel had not yet decided how to put the Negroes or whether the Third is to march in three columns or en masse. We are going to Scullyville,[1] will concentrate there, and then start again.

We started this morning about seven o'clock. Our order of march was as follows: I came first in the ambulance, followed by Errickson leading Zaidee, saddled and bridled and with a waterproof covering on the saddle. About a hundred yards behind came Alexander and the other officers, followed by their companies, with guidons flying. The company ambulances and wagons succeeded them, and the herd of beeves brought up the rear. Altogether we made quite an imposing display.

I presented quite a funny appearance. I was seated in a high rocking chair which was fastened by cleats to the bottom of the ambulance. Under my chair was my tin washbowl and pitcher (presented by Lieutenant Mulford); in front was a box of books (my traveling library), lunch basket, Andrew's and my bags, shawls, tin cups, a canteen of milk, one of water, etc., etc. Hanging from the top of the ambulance were two leather pockets, one of them containing my revolver, the other a field glass; a looking glass; my sewing basket; and a lantern also swayed to and fro. Indeed I cannot begin to enumerate the

various articles with which I was surrounded—a liquor case,
water cask, shotgun, carbine, Andrew's sabre and pistol, and
a dozen other things, and finally, before I had been under way
two or three hours, my compassion was imposed upon to such
an extent that I took in Flora, Sullivan's Newfoundland pup,
and Fan, who were both so tired with the unusual journey that
they were glad enough to lay quietly down in the bottom of the
ambulance, Fan under my feet—the only place for her. The
pups were put in one of the wagons, crying most vociferously,
and the wagon they were in turned over twice on the road,
greatly to the terror of the poor little fellows, who were more
frightened than hurt.[2]

We made a long march today, twenty-two miles, to Camp
Creek, the first place we could get water enough. We arrived
in the afternoon and found the first column in camp. Colonel
Van Vliet sent us an invitation to dine with him. We could not
go, as he was half a mile off and the horses were grazing, but
we asked him to send us our dinner, which he did, and [it]
was most acceptable. A novel way, I thought, to accept an invitation.

It was delightful to encamp in a new spot after the old
camp at Fort Smith where we had been so long. A square of
grass was cut first and then the tent pitched, and the odor of
"new-mown hay" was a great improvement on our late per-
fume, "essence de cheval." I slept long and soundly, undis-
turbed by my natural enemies the flies.

June 9

A number of Choctaws, half-civilized Indians, have come
around the camp; few of them could speak any English. It
was quite amusing to see the curiosity they excited in many
of these new recruits. We bought some dewberries of them.
All knew enough English to say "two bits" (twenty-five cents).

I lost my cook Rudolph today under rather amusing circumstances. He went off to an Indian camp near here to buy
some butter and eggs. While there the Indians gave him two
little polecats, which he brought home with him in triumph,

"for pets for Mrs. Alexander," putting them for safety in my tin lunchbox. He declared he thought they were young coons. The Indians undoubtedly gave them to him in perfect good faith, for they themselves raise these polecats for pets and are very fond of them for food.[3] They are very good eating, it is said, and resemble a young porker. The condition of my lunch box can be easily imagined, and Mr. Alexander was so incensed with him for putting them in there that he reduced him to the ranks and fetched me up another cook from the company.

Major Stanwood and Mr. Wilson dined with us, having come up in the third column, which arrived this afternoon. Just before sunset I went out for a ride with Andrew and Colonel Van Vliet. We shot a few quail. The Indians say there is plenty of deer in the neighborhood.

The wild flowers here are most brilliant. I recognize many of our garden flowers: spiderwort, purple verbenas, phlox, and larkspur. There are some handsome white flowers, the wild hyacinth, "cactis," and one, the most delicate of all, is the blossom of a thorny, sensitive plant. The flower is spherical and consists of little crimson filaments, half an inch long, radiating from the centre, and each crimson thread is tipped with a minute gold ball. I think this plant, with its sensitive leaves shrinking from the least touch, is one of the most delicate and beautiful plants I have ever seen. I only wish I had followed my mother's suggestion and brought my botany with me that I might classify these beautiful flowers. There are several of the pea variety, some yellow, some white, some pink and yellow—each, though, an entirely different plant. I am going to try and press some of these flowers, but I have few conveniences for doing so. They say we find abundant varieties of cacti. Those I have seen thus far were yellow or yellow tinged with scarlet in the middle. They were very handsome but frightfully uncomfortable to handle, as they were full of minute thorns which, though almost impossible to detect, were exceedingly painful.

The third column came in tonight with the Negroes. Colonel Howe and the Headquarters [Company] came with it.

June 10 Sunday
Camp Howe, near Scullyville

The first column moved off today, together with the headquarters, Colonel Howe having decided we were to move by
columns and that the Negro troops were to march a week with
the first column, then fall back and march a week with the
second and then a week with the third. After this time we
would be so far removed from civilization there will be no
danger of desertion, and they will either march together in
our rear or will go on to the first column.

We are to lay over every second Sunday. I only wish it
was to be every Sunday. It distresses me to travel on the Sabbath and to see the day so little regarded as it is in the army.

Before breakfast I met Colonel Van Vliet outside of my
tent; his face was beaming. He told me Colonel Howe had
transferred his Company C to our column in lieu of D (Cain
commanding) and that he and his lieutenant, Vroom, were
wild with delight. I am very glad of it, for I like Van Vliet and
Vroom better than any other of the officers. I do not know
them well but am pleased with what I have seen of them.
Vroom is a new appointment; [he] was in the volunteer army.
He has a good face and a fine soldierly bearing. They have been
very anxious to be transferred to this column, and I asked
Colonel Howe to change companies some two weeks ago when
he was gallantly extending the golden sceptre to me. They also
applied for a transfer two or three days ago, but the old man
did not think it practicable, and it was therefore a surprise to
all.

I have seen very little of the other officers of the column
excepting our Lieutenant Mulford, who messes with us, and
whom I like, and Lieutenant McMullen of A Company. He is
married, and they say his wife is a very pleasant woman and
well bred. As for Mr. McMullen, I should like him very well if
he had not forgotten himself so far as to be profane in my
presence, which I cannot but consider the greatest possible in-
sult a gentleman can offer one, and which I always resent.

We have no chaplain to this regiment, which I regret. I am

going to try and observe the Sabbath as much as possible. This morning about eleven o'clock Andrew and I had service. I have the Dutch church liturgy with me and read the lessons for the first Sabbath—the first chapter of Genesis and part of the first of John. Andrew read to me the first of the sermons of Bonar in the book Mama sent us for Christmas.[4] I am going to try and read one of these sermons every Sunday.

In the evening we walked over to see Mrs. Carroll (the baby bride). She looked very bright notwithstanding she had passed the night in the ambulance and her husband beneath it, the wagon containing her tent having been delayed. She is the only woman in the third column, and I am afraid she will be very lonely, poor child. I wish she was to be where I could look after her. Her husband belongs to G Company.

June 11

This morning we got fairly started on our trip. I made the first two hours and a half in the saddle. I rode with Andrew at the head of the column. I wore my black and white traveling dress [and] my black and white flat with a blue veil hanging around the edge. To give me a warlike appearance, I wore a miniature pistol belt with Jack's little pistol in a holster at one side and a silver-hilted dagger Colonel Van Vliet sent over to me at the other. This is to be my costume for crossing the plains.[5]

There are a great many jokes gotten off at the expense of my small pistol. Andrew declared I brought it to kill buffalo, at which Sullivan innocently remarked, "But Colonel, it would not go through a buffalo," and Andrew impertinently replied, "It might kill a fly on one." At the time of the Negro mutiny, one of the officers impertinently suggested that my pistol should be put in a carriage and dragged down to the scene of action to quell the disturbance.

We came about sixteen miles. The country through which we passed was much diversified: part of it was a rolling prairie and part woodland—in some places the Indians had ceased to burn over the prairie, and consequently it was covered with what is always the first growth on a prairie—a dwarf oak called "black jack" or "post oak." These oak barrens have a ragged appearance and look like the undergrowth which springs up in a forest where the trees have been cut away.[6]

We came across several Indian huts on our march. They looked very comfortless and were built either of logs, with the chinks unfilled, or were a loose shieldings of boards in the form of a wedge. By each of these hovels was a plot of ground under cultivation, usually surrounded by a rail fence and planted with potatoes, corn, beans, etc.

The Indians living in this part of the territory are the Creeks, Choctaws, and Cherokees. These tribes are semicivilized, but as we go further west we enter upon a vast tract of uninhabited country where even the Indian wigwam is not seen but which remains in all its original wildness, a great preserve, the hunting grounds of the Comanches, Kioways, Pawnees, and Apaches, fierce and independent tribes who have never as yet succumbed to the power of approaching civilization.

This country is watered by the Arkansas, the Canadian, the Red River, and other smaller streams and is traversed by herds of buffalo, wild horses, elk, and other smaller game. I am afraid the immense herds of buffalo will have gone north before we come to their region, as they winter here and in the northern part of Texas and go north in the summer.

Some parts of the country through which we passed today were very beautiful. I remember one place in particular where the fleeting shadows of the clouds were cast on a beautiful hill dotted with clumps of trees apparently left there by the artistic hand of a landscape gardener. The hill gradually sloped off into a magnificent lawn, the grass so bright, so even, one could hardly realize it had not just come from under the scythe and roller. A little further on we came to a fine grove, free from underbrush, but with several dead trees lying about, at which Andrew remarked, "The gentleman is neglecting his park." It was difficult to believe that the beautiful domain before us had never felt the touch of man but owed all its loveliness to the bountiful hand of nature.

We made about sixteen miles today and encamped at Coon Creek.

June 12

Camp Stoneman, Coon Creek, Indian Territory

This morning awoke in a rainstorm. The rain was so heavy that the road, which is low and boggy, became impassable for the wagons. Word was brought Andrew the first was immoveable in a mud hole, so he went down there with forty men who soon pulled the wagon out. It rained so heavily all the morning that we did not leave camp until ten o'clock.

I got very much disgusted with life this morning. When I got up I found my flat on the floor, the trimming off, the veil torn, and the brim partly chewed up by the pups. I was very outraged, for I cannot get another hat for love or money 'till I get to New Mexico, and probably not then.

I gave Andrew his old hat to wear so his new one should not get wet in the rain. When I went to make up the bed I found the blankets had fallen down back of the bed and consequently were wet, [and] pulling them up, I discovered Andrew's new hat full of water to the brim, as it had fallen just where it caught all the rain that ran off the tent. The climax was clapped by discovering beside it a new book Major Stanwood had lent me in such a condition as can better be imagined than described. So much for rain in camp.

We only came about eight miles today on account of the rain, which continued till about two o'clock. We passed through some beautiful oak openings. We are encamped on a charming spot. My tent faces a ridge of beautifully sloping hills dotted here and there with clumps of trees and looking in the distance as if they were covered with young grain. In the distance a field covered with yellow flowers adds to the illusion by its perfect resemblance to a crop of ripe wheat.

A deer ran through camp towards evening, which inspired a number with ardour for the chase. Andrew was out with several officers till dark, but all were unsuccessful. Had quail for dinner.

June 13

First Camp on Sans Bois

We only made about eight miles today on account of the excessively bad roads which detained the wagons. We came through several swamps and crossed the Sans Bois at a ford, and the water touched the bottom of the ambulance each time. The Sans Bois is a full, broad creek. We are encamped a little beyond it in a fine oak opening though which flows a rocky streamlet of pure spring water.

We have added to our comforts today by the acquisition of two good milch cows. One of [the] G horses got lame and was to have been shot, as he could not go along, but Mr. Mulford traded him off at a little settlement here for two small Indian cows—wild as hawks but fine animals.

Attending to this, he came across a court of Indians. There were about fifty there—Choctaws. From all accounts there must have been a mixture of their old rites with the new. A fire was smouldering in the middle of the wigwam. In front of it was the judge, a fine-looking man who spoke English very well. Before him was the prisoner. The jury were seated on a long log, while the judge, his clerk, and another, whose office I did not learn, had each the honor of a chair. On a table in front of them were books and writing materials.[7]

Lost one of our cows tonight trying to put a rope around her. She was so frightened she ran away and left her calf.

June 14

Have had a pretty rough time today. After having made five or six miles we came to a creek so much swollen by last night's rain as to be almost impassable. The horses got over well enough, but every wagon got stuck and had to be pulled up by the soldiers. I left the ambulance to its fate and crossed over on Zaidee under Colonel Van Vliet's care. I looked a funny enough figure crossing over. It rained, and I had my water-proof cloak on, the hood drawn partly over my jockey cap. My dress was fastened up carefully and my cloak tucked in all around so that the tips of my feet were alone visible, and they were well gathered up. I did not get wet, though the water was above the saddle girths. We camped a short distance from "Copper Creek."

June 15

Second Camp on Sans Bois

Colonel Van Vliet went ahead this morning with a detachment to prepare the road. These low bottoms through which we are now going are rendered almost impassable by the heavy rainstorms we have so frequently. Andrew spent all the morning at yesterday's ford getting the commissary train across. Had all the officers over to lunch with me.

We left camp about 2 P.M. and made but seven miles, encamping on the Sans Bois again. I don't know why it is called "Sans Bois," for it is a very well wooded stream. We get very discouraging accounts of the road ahead; for two miles it is just a morass, they say.

June 16

We marched this morning at five o'clock. There was every sign of a rainy day, but I concluded to try my fortunes on Zay, as it is not much fun going through bogs in the ambulance. It soon began to sprinkle, and Andrew tied a poncho around my waist. This, with my cloak, kept me quite dry. After going three miles we halted, and Andrew went back to look after the trains that were in the swamp we had passed through. As we were likely to be here several hours, I got into the ambulance. Very soon the rain poured down as I have never seen it before. The lightning was terrific and struck once right near us. In a few minutes the road had become a torrent, and the water in the morass so high that no further marching today was practicable. So we went into camp, and all our train is not yet on terra firma.

June 17 Sunday

Remained in camp today. The last of the train did not get clear of the bottoms until noon. In the afternoon we read one of Bonar's sermons from the text "To preach the acceptable year of the Lord."

June 18

We moved camp about ten and marched about three miles through a beautiful "champaign" country. We are camped now on the crest of a ridge—behind us rise some thickly wooded hills abounding in game; at their base runs a fine stream that supplies us with water; from our tent door extends a beautiful little prairie skirted by oak openings and diversified by occasional clumps of young trees. The total absence of underbrush, occasioned by prairie fires, gives the forests that surround us the appearance of parks in the highest state of cultivation, and it is this, coupled with the knowledge of our remoteness from all the busy haunts of men, that gives this country its greatest charm.

We heard today from the first column. Colonel Howe is only twelve miles from here, and most of his train is stuck in the mud about eight miles off. We have concluded to remain here until we know his column is again in motion. This is a very fine camping ground, but ahead of us there is another piece of bad road which will be improved by a day or two of sunshine.

I began father's slippers today; they are lilies of the valley with their leaves on a scarlet ground. I think they will be a pretty souvenir for him of my "tour of the prairies."

June 19

Alexander the mighty hunter started off at early dawn this morning with Colonel Van Vliet and Major Tarleton in quest of game. They returned about eleven and brought with them a beautiful young fawn, a *wolf pup*, and a large hawk. The latter met its death on account of its tail, which was a handsome brown, and Andrew thought [it] would look well on my hat. The young wolf was killed on principle and brought home for a curiosity. As for the fawn, it was a beautiful young creature, spotted regularly all over with white. It was shot through the head. I confess my bird hunting had not made me so hard-hearted but what I felt a pang for the beautiful creature. I sent word to have it carefully skinned and betook myself soon after to see it cut up properly. I begin to realize I have got into the law of the redmen, where the squaw has onerous duties to perform. Yesterday I was superintending the disjointure of a calf and today have performed the same office by a fawn.

Andrew wounded a fine doe, but it got away. He brought in a leg of a buck killed by one of the men in camp. This is the first day we have had any game excepting birds. As we go further into the country we shall find it in greater abundance.

Have been trying my hand at calf's-head soup. I invited Van Vliet and Vroom to dinner at 6 P.M.

June 20
Camp beyond Santa Rita Creek

Marched this morning at five o'clock; only made six miles, as we had another bottom to come through, and there is no need of haste, as the first column is reported to be but twelve miles in advance.

Colonel Van Vliet sent me some fish he had caught in the adjacent creek. We camped on a rocky oak ridge.

June 21
Camp at Gaines Creek

This morning, having concluded to avoid the bad road in our front by taking a new route, Andrew moved the column due north for five miles on a road he cut through the woods. We struck Beale's route and marched ten miles to Gaines Creek, where we are now encamped.[8]

While crossing through the timber, I was at one time far in the advance, Andrew having left with Errickson in attendance while he went back to the column. As I was waiting quietly on Zaidee, a fine black horse about fourteen hands high came trotting through the woods. It approached within fifty yards of me and then threw up its head and galloped off, mane and tail flying. I thought at the time it was a horse from the first column that had been lost and found its way back here, but could not see any brand on him, but the guide said it was a wild horse, there being a large drove in the vicinity. None of the officers saw him.

The third column came up this evening, having taken this road at the last crossing of the Sans Bois.

June 22
Camp 2½ miles beyond Gaines Creek

Crossed the creek, a broad, shallow, stream, this morning. The banks [on] each side were very steep and muddy. The bottom for three or four hundred yards was very bad. I crossed the creek and made our short march of 2½ miles in the ambulance—the pups and I were considerably knocked around and a little frightened as our conveyance veered from one side to the other. Andrew was wishing the other day Nelly was along. I thought of her today when we seemed within an ace of going over a dozen [times] and feared she would have found this a "harder road to travel" than the one General Stoneman's white mule carried her over.[9]

June 23

Marched eighteen miles today. At one time we were within three hundred yards of the Canadian; at this point we left Beale's road and struck south on the Texas route. Road very fine. I made half the distance on horseback. Left the road with Mr. Mulford just before getting into camp and ascended a curious hill, steep, round, and rocky, from which I got a magnificent view of the country.

June 24   Sunday

Made a march of about eighteen miles. Met several large droves, one a herd of three hundred horses, coming north from Texas. Encamped on a fine prairie.

June 25

This morning Andrew and I took the road about an hour before the column started and went off in search of quail. Rattler struck a deer trail, and we left the smaller game to follow this up. This was the first time I had seen a hound trail, and it interested me very much. The dog gives a quick bark and then smells along the ground. If he is on the trail of a deer he carries his head high and smells of the branches and trunks of the trees against which the deer has brushed, but if he is trailing a wild turkey he keeps his nose close to the ground. By this way we discovered this morning that Rattler was after a deer. As the grass was dry, the scent was faint, and sometimes he would appear to lose the trail. Then he would come to a spot where the deer had grazed around, and he would nose around for some time till at last he discovered where it had started on again, which he would announce by a succession of hoarse barks, and run on. As the trail became fresher he barked more frequently and ran on faster, Andrew and I following close behind. At last he came upon the game, and I saw for the first time a fine buck in its native woods. It started up from its lair, looked around for a moment, then bounded across the open country and was again under the shelter of the woodland. Andrew fired at it at about one hundred yards but was too far for a gun to take effect. We started another deer, too, on our way back to rejoin the column but did not get a shot at it.

We got back on the old road during the march. We have made somewhat of a divergence, increasing the length of our journey but escaping some very bad roads.

I began teaching Jacob, Andrew's "brevet bugler," to read today. He is a smart boy, about fourteen years old, though he declares he is eighteen.

Dr. Huntington made his appearance here this evening, having fallen back from the first column. He reports Colonel Howe thirty-five or forty miles ahead. There has been a good deal of sickness in the first column. Colonel Howe has been very sick; there has been a death and a *birth*—one of the laundresses in L company. The doctor takes up his quarters with us. He is very pleasant, and I like him as well as Comstock expected.

June 26

We came over some very bad roads today, and as I was in the ambulance, I was sufficiently jolted. The pups have gotten so large I have been obliged to throw away their box, and they roam at large in the ambulance. The first day I tried this they wanted to get out. Flos crawled up near the edge, and as we were going slowly, I gave her a push and out she fell. When she was put back again she had had enough of that and was perfectly quiet. Boots jumped out too, and that satisfied him. They have been very good since this lesson they got. We heard today though that Dick Wilson had fallen out of his wagon and broken his leg. His master is inconsolable. The leg has been set and splinted by the surgeon, and Dick has been swung in a box, but there are great fears that he will not recover.

June 27

Made about seventeen miles today and encamped on a large prairie near a fine stream of running water. The country begins to open up now; the prairies are more extensive and stretch on in great undulations interspersed here [and] there by small belts or clumps of timber.

Major Tarleton shot a fine doe this morning before we left camp. I watched him through the glass. The deer was browsing on the prairie at the edge of a wood, apparently unconscious of all danger. Andrew brought in a fawn. I am going to make a whip handle for myself and one for Emily of the forelegs.[10]

June 28

We made a march of about twenty miles today and encamped on the prairie by a small stream. In our march we traversed a prairie of about ten miles in extent—a broad, billowy waste of grass as far as the eye could reach. It was much finer than the prairies in Illinois or Indiana, as instead of being a dead level the land was diversified by undulations. From "Brogan's Store," which we passed during the day, I sent a letter home. This spot I believe is the last landmark of civilization.

We have left the Whipple route and are traveling south of it on the old Arbuckle road. We are about forty miles from Fort Arbuckle, they say.[11]

I take a new interest in the large anthills along the roadside, since Captain Hawley tells me garnets are often found there, thrown up by the ant in its excavations. He says he got from seventy to one hundred very fine garnets in the anthills south of the Rio Grande.

June 29

Made about fifteen miles over a very rough road and came to a sudden halt upon learning that the first column is but six miles in advance, being in camp on the Washita, which is unfordable. Encamped in an open meadow entirely surrounded by a belt of oaks. Found a tarantula's nest near our tent. They are very curious. They have a trapdoor at their entrance which is open when Mr. Tarrantula is away from home, but which by some singular mechanism closes after him when he enters his hole. A passage a couple of inches wide leads to his nest, which is found about two feet underground and which is lined with silk softer and more beautiful than the silkworm's cocoon. There have been some immense tarantulas found. The largest I have seen had a body the size of a hickory nut and long thick legs covered with hair. They are mammoth spiders and very poisonous. One of the I Company men was bitten by one a couple of weeks ago and is still laid up with it. Mr. Vroom found one in his blanket the other night.

It would be quite curious to keep a record of the strange bedfellows our misery has made some of us acquainted with on this trip. I have found nothing worse than a treefrog in my bed, but someone else had a visit from a lizard, and one of the wagoners felt something move at his feet the other morning and discovered a couple of little polecats snugly ensconced there.

June 30

Remained in camp all day. Some of the officers rode over to the first column and brought back melancholy accounts of the condition of things there. Colonel Howe is in great terror of the Comanches, will not even permit an officer to go hunting for fear of getting him scalped, and insists upon sending a guard with everyone who goes a mile or two from camp. He talks of concentrating the regiment, which is not a pleasant suggestion to the second and third columns. From all accounts everyone in the first column leads a dog's life. Colonel Howe starts them off at daylight, he taking the lead *in his carriage.*

July 1   Sunday

Moved about two miles to a better camp early in the morning and laid over all day. The third column camped alongside of us.

July 2

A sad accident occured this morning about seven o'clock. One of the soldiers was cleaning his pistol carelessly when it went off and killed instantly a soldier standing by, a G Company man called Edmund Ryan. They brought me his pocket book and watch to put away. He was a good soldier, and his sudden death was deeply felt by the men. He was buried at noon. Andrew had his grave dug in a little grove close by the foot of a large oak. The body was sewed up in canvas and carried on a stretcher by four soldiers. Then came G Company followed by Andrew and some of the other officers. I watched them from the door of my tent, and never has the burial of a stranger affected me so deeply. Andrew read the funeral service from my prayer book at the grave, then the "uncoffined clay" was lowered, and three volleys of musketry proclaimed that a soldier had found his last resting place. I rode over to see his grave afterward; a tablet had been cut into the living monument at the head, and in the wood was deeply engraved a cross, the initial of his name, company, and regiment.

July 3

Yesterday late in the day we marched about nine miles to a new camp, as we had received orders to keep within "supporting distance" of the first column, which moved early in the day. This morning we left at our usual hour, and after marching ten miles came to the place where Colonel Howe had encamped the night before. We proceeded with the intention of encamping six or eight miles ahead, but our day's march was not over until we had gone *forty-five* miles![12] We found ourselves on an extensive prairie utterly devoid of water. The day's march was most wearisome and particularly harassing to Andrew, who had the care of the command. He had men out constantly looking for water two or three miles from the road. We found a pool of muddy water where the men filled their canteens, and another nearby where the horses got a little drink, but this was all, and the mules and cattle did not get a mouthful till the next morning. Colonel Howe had sent us back no intimation of this, and it was so utterly unlooked for that the water casks were not even filled. All we could do was to push on until we got to where the first column was encamped.

Soon after dark I became sleepy and, pushing the dogs aside, laid down on their blanket on the bottom of the ambulance. The pups revenged themselves by stretching themselves across me while Fan lay curled up at the top of the ambulance with her head on my pillow. Pointers are the cleanest things that walk on four legs, so I did not mind their company, and we dozed together quite comfortably until near midnight, when we reached Colonel Howe's camp. Here we found just a little water for the men, but learned there was a creek about three miles off, and the road to it was being repaired in the night, as there was a deep arroyo to pass. We went supperless and disgusted to bed.

July 4

In the morning at sunrise we started again, without breakfast, and marched to the creek. The road was obstructed by Colonel Howe's train, and we were over three hours in getting there with the wagons. We found a running stream of water and the poor animals at last got watered, and about half past nine we had our breakfast, the first we had had excepting a few crackers for thirty hours.

We find that Colonel Howe was as ignorant as we of the road. In fact he had been lost for some time. He started on Whipple's route and wandered off, and when he was encamped on the Washita was within thirty miles of the border of Texas. We were right when we were on Beale's road, but of course have to follow our chief. When he left the Washita, day before yesterday, he quarreled with his guide, an old Comanche. He had engaged his services at five dollars a day, the chief wanted it in silver, Colonel Howe insisted on greenbacks, and as the Indian of course would not take it, concluded to *guide the column himself with a compass!* His economy was a sorry one for the government, for yesterday's march cost the government, in wear and tear of stock, thousands of dollars. The one mule that we lost would have paid him over and over again, and that was probably the first victim only.[13]

We remembered the Fourth this morning as we rode breakfastless along and sighed for roast pig and its concomitants with which those at home were celebrating the day. However, after breakfast we felt more cheerful. The whole command were asleep pretty much all day, which was hot, as the Fourth usually is. About noon, after we had taken a long nap, Andrew and I became a little frisky and had a political meeting, or rather a social gathering, at which, after describing the imaginary surroundings, I called upon Andrew to respond to the toast, "The day we celebrate." He began his address with great elegance, apologizing for his costume which was rendered advisable not only by the heat of the weather but by the customs of the people through whose land we were passing. As I was the large audience, I of course had to applaud from time to time with energy; and part of the speech, if it failed to bring down the house, brought down the *bed.* Andrew told me a most amusing anecdote of the "First Indian Cavalry."

On the whole we passed quite a comfortable Fourth and drank to its many returns in a large tin cup of lemonade. We dined about seven: had tomato soup, wild turkey, beefsteak, green peas, and canned peaches for desert—Dr. Huntington and Mr. Mulford, Andrew and I. We remembered the Croquet family, July, '65.[14]

July 5

Moved camp about two miles in the afternoon. In the evening there was the most gorgeous rainbow in the heavens I have ever seen. It was a perfect arc and the colors most brilliant, and the secondary bow, though faint, was also distinguishable from end to end. The sunset was also uncommonly beautiful.

July 6

This morning a courier came from Colonel Howe informing us we were on the wrong road and he was going to cut across country to another trail. This information excited more mirth than indignation in our column, for we expected little else from our guide, the Colonel—"We knew not the way we are going but too well we know our guide"—to expect anything else than that we shall vibrate between the Washita and Canadian as we have been doing.

We retraced our steps to yesterday's camp and then pursued our way along an Indian trail, well grown over. I made the march (about ten miles) on horseback, riding somewhat in advance of the column with Andrew and Colonel Van Vliet. During our ride in a ravine we came across a couple of wildcats, a species of panther and very "game birds." Colonel Van Vliet shot one with his rifle, and while this was going on I slid down from my horse, took a pistol, and killed the other, a young cub, that had run up into a tree near me. Andrew insisted upon addressing me the rest of the day as "Eveline, the great panther killer of the prairie."

The skins were very pretty, spotted all over, but were so full of ticks we threw them away. When the pups saw the skins they were very much frightened and ran howling away. Curious instinct.

We were a good deal distressed in the evening by the absence of Jacob, Andrew's "brevet bugler." He had gone off with a message to Andrew, who was hunting across the prairie, and we feared he was lost. He came in, though, just at dark, having heard the carbines that were fired for him. Andrew killed a grey eagle.

July 7

This morning started off in a steady rain which cleared up, however, about noon. I met with a funny accident last

night. I turned over once too often in my sleep and found myself on the grass beneath the eaves of the tent. I scrambled up
into bed again in a hurry, thinking of snakes and tarantulas.

July 8

Marched about sixteen miles and found ourselves once
more on the False Washita and, they say, only twenty-five
miles further up than when we left it the 2nd of July, which
is not very encouraging, to say the least.

I saw some Caddo Indians; they have a reservation about
here.[15] They were half-civilized and wore clothes; one of them
had on a gay dressing gown, a bright, beaded kerchief bound
around his head, and was painted in stripes running from the
tip of his ear to the mouth, black and vermilion.

July 9

Made a short march of twelve or fourteeen miles and
camped at Fort Cobb, where we found the first column. This
post was abandoned the first year of the war, and nothing remains but the ruins of a few houses that were burnt.[16]

Lieutenant and Mrs. Sutorius came over and dined with
us in the evening. This is the first I have seen of them since we
started on the march.

July 10

We laid over today that the first battalion might get a
day in advance of us. Andrew went hunting and brought home
a fine turkey and said he came across the largest buck he had
ever seen but did not get a shot at it. Fresh tracks of buffalo
have been found around camp, and all are getting excited over
the prospect of coming across these mighty denizens of the
prairie.

Dr. Huntington and I started off in search of a prairie dog
village that we heard was in the vicinity but took the wrong
direction and did not find it. When we returned, we called up
Sullivan (Andrew's body servant), who is an old soldier and
well acquainted with prairie life, and asked him for some particulars respecting the abode of the prairie dogs. His descrip-

tion of their habitations was most amusing. The entrance to them was a "round circle, about a foot square just in the top of the mound."

Sullivan is a great character; he has always been "striker" to the officer commanding the company and is consequently perfectly worthless. He never does anything right, or twice in the same way, and the only reason Andrew does not send him back to the company is that he is useless there. He occasionally gets off some very fine "bulls" like the above mentioned. I remember when we were at Fort Smith, Andrew saw a horse fall and sent Sullivan down to inquire [into] the matter. He returned to say a picket pin had struck the horse "and knocked him *speechless*, sir!"

III

Across the Buffalo Plains

Fort Cobb to Fort Union, July–August, 1866

July 11

Marched about sixteen miles. Just after reaching camp a heavy thunderstorm came up, and the rain fell in sheets. One bolt, accompanied by a terrific report, struck close to us, and in a moment more A, G, and I companies had stampeded and were careening over the hills. One must have been some time with a cavalry regiment to appreciate the excitement of a stampede. It is the greatest trouble one has to apprehend, and the danger of it is often discussed, and every effort made with picket pins or hobbles and guards to provide against it.

The greater part of the horses were turned after they had run about five miles. Zay came very near being killed. She was at the head of the "fast stock," a herd of about a dozen horses that had outrun the rest. Lieutenant Russel had his pistol raised to shoot her, as in a stampede if you shoot the leader the rest will usually stop, but he fortunately recognized her as my horse and succeeded in turning her, and she was caught on her way back. I rather disgusted Andrew by saying if my horse was to run, I was glad that she distinguished herself and beat the rest of the regiment.

It is singular what a frenzy seizes horses during a stampede. Old broken-down things that can hardly drag one foot after the other will run forty or fifty miles and drop down dead. Their eyes become glazed and blurred after they run awhile, and sometimes they run into a river and drown. By night all but eight of the horses were recovered, and these were found the next day.

July 12

Our march today was rainy, as we had a succession of little showers. Two antelope were seen near the road and a flock of wild turkeys. We also had our first view of buffalo. Several herds of a dozen or so were seen browsing about a mile off. Our guide killed one, and we had a steak off a buffalo rump for dinner. It tasted very little different from beef.

July 13

Marched eleven miles; the road crossed over several very wild, rocky ravines. I left the column and went [to] one side about half a mile to see a buffalo Colonel Van Vliet had killed. Zay was rather afraid of it, as all horses are. It was a buffalo bull, and an immense great creature with short black horns and a huge mane and beard. I would like to have seen him on the run with his great tongue hanging out and his little eyes blazing.

We passed through a prairie dog village, but none of the inhabitants showed themselves. We hear from the first column that Colonel Harwood of the colored regiment went hunting yesterday morning and has not been heard of since. Scouts were out looking for him.

The water at this camp is epsom and very disagreeable and bad for the men.

July 14

Marched nine miles only and came across the first column, still in camp. They are awaiting news from Colonel Harwood, and Colonel Howe has at last sent two companies from the first and ordered two from the second and third columns to go in search of him. There are fears he has been "gobbled up" by the Indians. This is the third day of his absence, and if he has not been captured by them, he has probably starved to death by this time, as they say he is not a man of many resources.[1] Andrew sent twenty-five men from C and the same from G Company on the search under Van Vliet and Russel. They have four days' rations issued to them, and we are to remain here and wait for them.

A charming day—a fine breeze blowing which cools the air delightfully. We are once more on the Whipple route, they say, though all in this column feel very uncertain where they are.

This evening we had quite an excitement over a large herd of buffalo which was making for this creek where we are encamped. We were afraid they would run into camp and stampede the horses. A number of men were stationed at the creek to keep them away by firing carbines. It was too dark to see how many there were, but by the noise of their trampling and bellowing we concluded there were five or six hundred.

July 15   Sunday

We spent the day very quietly in camp. In the afternoon we had a little excitement. A Company's horses, who were picketed [on] the other side of the creek where we were encamped, came tearing across the creek, and at their heels a large buffalo. He had evidently been near, got away from the herd, and was bewildered, for he ran right through our camp and over the hill, passing within one hundred yards of where I stood. This was the nearest view we have had of a buffalo. We saw large herds around during the day.

July 16

We did not move camp until late in the afternoon, and then we only went a couple of miles to a new camp on the Washita, where we found better water. The water at this last camp was a dilution of epsom salts and very disagreeable.

Andrew killed a "jackass-rabbit" today. They are very curious; they look like the English hare, but have a pair of long, delicate ears at least twice the length of their head, and they run like the wind.

The parties out in search of Colonel Harwood returned this evening having been unsuccessful. The poor man has doubtless met his death before this—either by starvation or the Indians. "Lost on the prairies!"—what sad tidings to give to his friends!

We have seen not an Indian for two weeks. This makes us think they are hostile, for if they are, and have been committing depredations on the northern route, we will not see a sign of one.

July 17

Marched about eighteen miles and had an interesting day of it. Andrew started off early with about twenty men to hunt buffalo for the column, which will keep up our [cattle] herd in numbers. They killed eight during the day. We must have seen a thousand buffalo during the march. In every direction, as far as we could see, great herds of buffalo were grazing, and Andrew says they were the tamest he ever saw. Several times squads of half a dozen ran right in front of the column as we marched, and once a larger herd was just making for us when half a dozen men galloped off and by shouting turned them.

Just as we were leaving camp in the morning, Mr. Vroom rode up to me and directed my attention to a herd of buffalo who had crossed over the Washita and were in the rear of our camp going northerly. I thought this was too good an opportunity to be lost, so, calling to Mr. Mulford, we started for the herd. As we got near, Zay scented them and snorted. The wind was high, and as we galloped on, off flew my hat and net, but we picked them up and I held them in my hand, and we continued on our course. We made a short cut by a hill and came up within fifty yards of the buffalo. There were about thirty in the herd; the cows and calves were in the advance, and an old bull with a long beard brought up the rear. He stopped and turned and looked at us, and then he gave warning, I suppose, for the herd began their headlong gallop and were soon out of sight. I have been trying to think what they look like when they gallop and decided it is like a drove of hogs on a full run, as they go where one beats them. In the distance they have just that headlong, walloping movement, and their short legs and immense bodies add to the effect and remind you of a drove of wild black hogs.

I saw five antelope today. None were killed.

July 18

This morning I started off with the hunting party, but the buffalo that were so plentiful yesterday had most of them disappeared; or rather we could see them in the distance beyond the Washita. We came across two or three small herds but were unsuccessful. Had a run with an old buffalo bull. Andrew fired one shot at him, but the hammer of his pistol was broken, so he had to give it up.

At present it is as if we were passing through an enemy's country. We have to have pickets out at night, who fire at the approach of the buffalo, and at the sound the whole camp is in commotion. This afternoon we were asleep when a cry of "buffalo!" sounded. Andrew sprang up and rushed out under the side of the tent in his stocking feet and without waiting for his hat and in a moment more was on the hill thundering out commands. There was a herd of some thirty or forty making direct for the camp. By dint of yelling and firing of carbines they were turned away from the horses and tents and rushed down between the camp and a herd of mules.

This lookout for buffalo is quite exciting. Last night we heard something rushing down through camp and Andrew sprang out of bed and pulled me out after him, intending to put me *under* the bed for protection, for he thought the buffalo were upon us, and they would just rush over a tent in a moment. However this was a false alarm and proved to be only some mules that had got loose.

July 19

We did not move till late in the afternoon, then marched fifteen miles to a pond of tolerable water. We marched an hour or two by moonlight, and once, just after sunset, as we were going up a hill, we came suddenly upon a herd of buffalo. The column came to a sudden halt, which was more than the buffalo did; they broke over the hill first, then turned and came back, but were at last driven aside by firing at them and yelling. The difficulty is when one sees a few buffalo appearing over the crest of the hill, one never knows if it is a small herd or a thousand or more who are upon us. My ambulance was sent in [the] rear of the first company for the rest of the march.

July 20

We marched eleven miles, leaving camp early in the morning, and came upon the Canadian River, and right glad we were to see it too, for in truth for the last fortnight we have been very much at a loss to determine in what part of the Indian Territory we were or whether we had not wandered into Texas and were near the Staked Plain.

We are now once more on Whipple's route, at Camp 36, Canadian River. The Canadian presents now the broad, sandy bed of a river with here and there a little water. The water sinks and runs under the sand, they say.

We remained four of five hours on the Canadian and let the horses graze, then continued our journey in the afternoon. We passed between the "Antelope Buttes," which you will see on the map and [which] are near the line dividing the Indian Territory and the upper part of Texas. These buttes are very curious. They are high tables of rock, perfectly flat on top as all buttes are, with very precipitous sides.[2] On the top of the highest butte was a pole with something hanging from it and waving in the wind which, exciting our attention, Andrew sent a man up after it. He succeeded in scaling the butte and returned a human scalp, dried and stretched within a small reed hoop! It was fastened securely to the pole by thongs of buckskin. It was evidently, from the color and texture of the hair, a white woman's scalp. This much we determined upon.

July 21

We had another deliberation today over the scalp (which is tied to the ambulance). We had the guides up, and from what they said came to the conclusion it was the scalp of a little girl about twelve years old whom the Indians captured along with her brother some months ago in Texas. The boy was brought into a post by some half-civilized Comanches and ransomed for one hundred dollars. [They] went back for the girl but returned and said that Buffalo Hump, the great

Comanche chief, would not give her up. And that was the last heard of her. This was probably her scalp—the hair was dark brown, short, and fine but had been neglected lately. Whether they had a great war dance on this butte, killed the girl, and put her scalp up there for medicine, or whether they had suspended this white scalp on this conspicuous point in our path as a token of defiance to us, we did not determine.[3] I inclined to the latter. However, my thoughts rested little on the tragic fate of this child during the day, for they were taken up with a grief that came nearer home.

We have lost our dear old Fan. Last night when we got into camp we found she was not with us, and Andrew remembered that he had not seen her since they passed a spring some four miles back. She had got very tired and was lying down by the roadside. (I was unfortunately on another road with the ambulance.) Andrew thought of course she would come on and did not think of her again till we got into camp, which was late, as we had marched in all twenty-seven miles. Then he began to inquire about her and found one of the men had last seen her at this spring about four miles from camp, and he thought from her appearance she had a fit. We looked for her coming all night, and at daylight Andrew's First Sergeant Armstrong went back to this spring and searched everywhere for her, but in vain. Poor dear Fan, the best we can hope for her is that she died in a fit and that the wolves only found her dead body. I have been grieving for her all day.

I tried to divert myself by putting a black band around Flo's and Jack's necks as mourning for their mother, but unsuccessfully, and when I thought of Fan and her devotion to Andrew, and her beautiful head and eyes, and then pictured her in a death struggle with one of these frightful wolves that howl around the camp at night, I found myself a dozen times on the point of crying as I did when I heard of Max's death.[4] And I will confess to my journal that in the dark a few tears did fall on little Flossy's head when she came nestling up to me. Andrew says little about his lost favorite, excepting once or twice when he has remarked, "After all she was a dog." He says it I think more to himself than to me.

We marched today twenty-three miles and encamped by the first column near the "mouth of Wolf Creek."

July 22   Sunday

Passed the day very quietly in camp. It was a hot day, and we were glad not to be on the march. Two Indians were seen during the day. They appeared over the crest of the hill, evidently came upon the camp unexpectedly, and dashed off again. There seems to be no longer a doubt that the Comanches are hostile. They are the most numerous of any of the Indian tribes.[5] This is their tract that we are passing through now, and today was the first sign we have seen of one.

I am much disappointed at not seeing the bands of wild Indians that usually throng the camp, for I had made extensive preparations for trading with them in the shape of red cloth, beads, and trinkets.

July 23

Marched twenty miles and camped on the Canadian. Opposite our camp on the other side of the Canadian was a line of buttes of most singular formation; there was a regularity about their lines that gave them all the appearance of fortifications. I tried to sketch the outline. The sun set immediately in the rear of them and added beauty of color to the strange scene.

We are now passing through Texas, and at present are passing along the line of the Canadian. Colonel Howe is making long marches now, for we are getting nearer to the end of our rations than to our journey's end. He is still *very* much on the alert for Indians. He told me Saturday he had ninety-five men (!) on guard in the first column, and sure enough, when we approached their camp we found them stretched in a regular cordon around camp extending ten or twelve miles. We have only twenty-five on guard in our column.

We passed through several prairie dog villages during the day. They are very numerous along the Canadian. They chose for the site of their villages a sandy level, covered with the buffalo grass so abundant in this part of the country. This buffalo [grass] is short, growing in patches, three or four inches high, and is very nutritious, as is also the gramma grass which begins to be very plentiful now.

As we passed through a prairie dog village the other day, we saw numbers of the burrowing owls that share the prairie dogs' houses with them. The owls were flying around or perched on the side of the hillocks or emerging from them. They did not seem as shy as their friends who drop so quickly into their holes on your approach that I have not had a satisfactory look at one yet.

July 24

Marched nearly twenty miles today and encamped again on the Canadian. We have probably seen our last of buffalo; the signs of them are becoming indistinct. Their "wallows" and "trails" are overgrown with weeds. The country for many miles has been ploughed up with the deep furrows they make in traveling, as they always follow one another in single file and leave a deep trail behind them. We have, however, marched one hundred miles at least in the last five days and have passed out of their tract.

The grass is quite dry in some places, and we have to guard against fires. We have found Colonel Howe's old camp on fire several times. Last week when we came up we found about one hundred acres in flames, and as it was burning when we left, it may have been an extensive fire before long. The flames were crawling along the grass, running thin tongues in and licking up every green twig.

The nights are charming now, very dry, and bright moonlight. After dinner (at seven) we lay on the grass in front of the tent a couple of hours enjoying the moon, the cool, dry breeze, and receiving whoever happens to drop in (or rather down).

July 25

Made about fifteen miles. The marching is telling upon many of our horses and mules; we have lost several of both.

Jack and Flos are growing amazingly every day. They look very pathetic with their necks circled with broad black bands. I suppose poor Fan brought at least fifty pups into the world, and these are the only ones who mourn for her. Colonel Van Vliet apologizes for Boots not appearing in black by telling me a pair of black pantaloons was all he had to cut up for the "usual mourning badges."

July 26

Marched only ten miles and again encamped on the Canadian. The river is rising a little, and the sand is now covered with water. Zaidee will not touch this water, and none of the horses like it, it is so thick with mud.

We have a fine breeze every day, which is invaluable during these warm marches. The winds across these plains blow with all the regularity of the trade winds—in summer from the southwest and in winter from the northwest.

It was hard traveling today for the animals; the roads were very deep sand. We are now nearing the boundary of New Mexico, and directly south of us stretches the Staked Plain, so called from a road the Spaniards made across it which in the absence of all landmarks was indicated by stakes driven in along the route.[6] In following Whipple's course, we travel about thirty-five miles on the Staked Plain, crossing its extreme northern boundary, but I believe we are to leave Whipple's route here ("last camp on Canadian") and take some other line, probably north of the Canadian.

July 27

We marched five or six miles and came suddenly upon the first column encamped on the other side of the Canadian.[7] Upon inquiry we found they had continued on Whipple's route (which here crosses the Staked Plain) for two or three miles, but found the road impassable almost on account of the sand which was two and one-half feet deep and in which the wagons sank up to their hubs. As their scouts found no signs of water for some distance ahead, Colonel Howe retraced his steps to the Canadian, intending if possible to strike Abert and Peck's route,[8] which runs north of this river to Fort Union.

We encamped alongside of the first column. It was one of the hottest days I have ever known. The wind which blew all day was like the breath of the sirocco, so hot and dry that when it struck you it fairly burnt your flesh.

July 28

Remained in camp until 3 P.M. then marched six miles. The day was as insufferably hot as yesterday, with the same hot wind. There was not a thermometer in the regiment, so we could not tell how hot we were. It was too hot to wear a dress, and during the march I rode in the ambulance in a white wrapper and managed to survive.

July 29   Sunday

Another very warm day; we marched [left blank] miles and encamped by good water but no wood except what we brought from the last camp. When we hear we are to camp without wood, we have a log of cottonwood fastened under each wagon and thus take our fuel with us.

Towards evening, as Andrew was reading to me one of Guthrie's sermons on the parables, signs of a thunderstorm made their appearance, and "the recall" was sounded and the horses tied up to the picket line in anticipation thereof. We were at dinner when the storm burst upon us in all its fury. We swallowed " a hasty plate of soup" (vide Scott's memoirs), and then I made for my tent, as the cook tent looked rather insecure. I had Andrew's rubber cloak on me and ran close behind Andrew but nevertheless got thoroughly wet, and barely had I sheltered myself before a terrific blast of wind and rain came, and in a moment the cook tent and every other tent in the column excepting mine was done. Andrew had taken extra precautions with the guys and iron pins which kept ours up. It did him little good, however, for though after some vivid flash of lightning he would run in to reassure me, he would be out again in a moment to see if the tent pins were all right and watch for the first signs of a stampede, for, as he said, at any moment a horse might switch up his tail and all be gone.

Everyone agreed it was one of the most terrific storms they had ever seen. We were encamped on a sandy ridge without a tree or a hill to shelter us from the fury of the storm. "The rains descended, and the floods came and the winds blew." I thought of this parable as I sat in my tent and moralized upon the downfall of the tents around us. All the dogs had taken shelter under my bed.

July 30

Marched fourteen miles over heavy sandy roads. During the day we struck a well-worn trail which we conclude is Abert's and Peck's. It is satisfactory to know we are not the first white people who have traveled this route.

July 31

Marched twenty-two miles. The greater part of our journey was over a tableland, perfectly level and entirely destitute of water and trees, but the road was the finest imaginable, and the wagons were no longer on the march today than yesterday. We all indulge in speculations as to our locality, but with no general conclusion. We think we have crossed into New Mexico, undoubtedly, but how near we are to our journey's end is a mere conjecture. The officers who have kept tally say we have traveled over eight hundred miles in our wanderings, and we all expected the close of this month would see us at Fort Union. I am beginning to believe we are to wander in this wilderness forty years or more until we have expiated the sins of the regiment, or until this generation shall have died off.

August 1

A delightful cool day, and we had a pleasant march of ten miles to where Colonel Howe camped last night. Our marches at present are quite irregular, as they have to be governed by the water, which is very scarce through this part of the country. Tomorrow we march twenty-two miles again to water, I believe, and are to carry our wood with us. There are a number of trees here by these pools of water—cottonwood—the only trees excepting evergreens that grow in New Mexico.[9]

August 2

Last night about nine o'clock, as we were going to bed, we heard a sudden rushing of horses' feet followed by the ever startling cry, "Stand to horse!" Another stampede. C Company was stopped on the onset as they happened to make to- wards camp, but the other companies were off. Andrew was out till after midnight hunting them and got in all but fifteen of the G horses, including Tom and Zay. This morning he started off again on the search, and by afternoon all the horses were recovered. It was an excessively hot day. We left camp about 3 A.M. and marched nine miles.

August 3

Left camp at 6 A.M. and marched fourteen miles. En- camped by some pools of water.

August 4

Marched eighteen miles. The road heavy.

August 5   Sunday

This morning, having marched about twelve miles, we came upon the Canadian again, or rather the "Red River" or "Rio Colorado," as it is called here in New Mexico.[10] The river has quite a different aspect from what it has lower down; it is very much narrower and bordered by high cliffs. We found very fine springs coming out of the rocks close by the road where we struck the river, but there was not the least grass for the animals, so after remaining here four or five hours while the men cooked their dinner and the animals rested, we marched six miles more and came into camp about sun- down.

August 6

Left camp this morning at an early hour, as we had a long march before us for water. After going 11 miles we came to Utah Creek, which we recognized with a great deal of interest as it was a landmark. We have not known within a hundred miles how near we were to Fort Union, but this creek we knew to be about 20 miles from Fort Bascom, which is 120 from Union. I think most of us were rather disappointed not to find ourselves nearer our journey's end, for many of the officers thought we had passed Utah Creek.

We made a long march today of twenty-four miles and encamped on the south side of the Red River near a Mexican ranch, the first we had seen. We learned that we were four miles from Fort Bascom.[11] Quite an excitement was occasioned among the soldiers, who did not know they were near any post, by the appearance of a "lady on a horseback" dressed in the usual costume of civilization. It proved to be Mrs. De Weisse,[12] the surgeon's wife, who had ridden down from the post with one of the officers to call on me and ask me to spend the day with her tomorrow if we remained over. She was a pretty, well-mannered woman such as one is surprised to find in the wildwoods.

August 7

Marched to Fort Bascom—four miles—in the morning, where we remained two or three hours. The officers thought this a very nice looking post. The officers' quarters were all adobe houses, so called from the bricks they are made of, which are only mud baked in the sun. The post is garrisoned by three companies of Mexicans, part of Kit Carson's regiment. They say they make very good soldiers when officered by white men as this is. Two of the companies were off with the colonel on a peace mission to the Comanches. The fort was under the command of Major Quintana, the only Mexican among the officers, I believe.[13]

I made Mrs. De Weisse a visit while we remained at the fort. Her husband, Dr. De Weisse, has gone on this expedition. She told me he was from Albany, a cousin of the Cornings. She was from New Jersey.

I called upon the major's wife, as that was etiquette, found her an exceedingly ugly Mexican lady who could speak no English. Mrs. De Weisse says she is very pleasant, however, the former having already picked up sufficient Spanish during the four months she has been here to make herself understood. Major Quintana spoke English very well and was exceedingly courteous.

When I started to call upon Mrs. Quintana, Mrs. De Weisse offered to lend me a *hoop skirt*, thinking probably I

would feel more at my ease, but I declined it, telling her it was
so long since I had worn a hooped skirt I was sure I should
feel awkward in it. It looked very curious to me to see a woman
again with ample skirts and with her hair fashionably arranged.

We camped about ten miles beyond the fort at "old Camp
Jackson."

August 8

Marched eleven miles and encamped for the last time on
the Red River,[14] which from this point runs to the northwest
of us. We are getting now into a mountainous country, and one
has only to look at the high hills around us to know that they
are the spurs of the *Rocky* Mountains. The surface of the
mountains is covered with immense boulders of rock that look
as if they had been thrown there by some gigantic power and
there stuck.

August 9

Marched twelve miles. Plenty of wood, water, and grass
when we camped.

August 10

Today we made fifteen miles and encamped on a stream
of water than runs into the Canadian. We received the satisfactory intelligence by courier from the first column that we
are but fifty-seven miles from Fort Union. We will get there
probably in four days. For the last fortnight everyone has felt
very impatient to get to the journey's end, not to speak of the
eagerness and anxiety with which we look forward to the letters that are awaiting us. The rations are getting low, the
horses thin, and the mules exhausted. We have had a very
fine trip, pleasant weather, and good water all along, but we
are nevertheless glad to be nearing the end of it.

August 11

Marched fifteen miles and encamped on a stream under a
grove of fine cottonwoods in the vicinity of a Mexican ranch.

The Mexican brought some green corn, cabbages, and milk as a present to "El Coronel," and in return Andrew gave him some tobacco and bought some onions and green peppers of him. The Mexican onions and "chili colorado" are the most noted productions of New Mexico; at least they have a great reputation among the officers who have lived here. This Mexican, however, had only "chili verde," with which we had to content ourselves.

This last week I have taken up my Spanish again with renewed interest and have already learned a great many words. Several old soldiers who have been out here before speak Mexican with a great deal of fluency; even old Sullivan seems able to make himself understood. Colonel Howe camped here yesterday and did not leave till late this morning on account of a general stampede of horses and mules which took place in his column last night.

The Mexicans appeared very much disgusted with the coming of the Negroes. They said when their women saw them they covered up their heads and ran behind the house crying, "All as black like night." These Negroes of the Fifty-seventh Regiment are indeed the most hideous blacks I have ever seen. There is hardly a mulatto among them; almost all are coal black, with frightfully bad places. They must have been the refuse from the other states, for when Negroes were incorrigible they were sold south to the cotton plantations of Arkansas and Louisiana.[15]

August 12

Our march today was the most beautiful of our route. The road led over the mountains, and as we ascended we could look down upon the country we had passed over for miles around. The atmosphere is so clear here that you can see to a great distance and are constantly deceived as to the proximity of different points. A hill that seems to be half a mile away, upon traveling you will find to be four or five miles distant.

This afternoon we watched a thunderstorm coming for an hour before it reached us. We could see it covering one mountaintop after another, while we still lay in the sunshine. We had Bierstadt's "Storm in the Rocky Mountains" in the original today.[16]

We are encamped tonight in a bright, level valley, surrounded on all sides by mountains that raise their lofty heads protectingly over our comp. Now that we are in this picturesque country, I am no longer tired of marching.

It is right cold here in these valleys. I have been chilly all day though I had my broadcloth jacket on. A curious complaint to make in August.

August 13

This morning we began our march by ascending a mountain for about six hundred feet. Everyone but I walked up; I rode Zay. It was so steep the wagons were three or four hours in getting up. We found a broad plain before us on coming to the top. I was looking for a descent, but Andrew laughed and said we would go downhill when we crossed the Rockys and descended towards California.

We had a long march of twenty-four miles and encamped within seven miles of Fort Union.

August 14
Fort Union[17]

We struck our tents at an early hour, for all were anxious to get to Fort Union and their letters. On our way we passed a ranch called "Barclay's Fort," which presented a singular appearance. It was surrounded by an adobe wall with round bastion towers at each end and had quite a massive gateway in front surmounted by a flagstaff. This was of older date than Fort Union and had been built as a defence against the Indians. The bastion towers (which were somewhat battered) have now been appropriated by the pigeons, who have built their nests in the loopholes.[18]

After riding about two hours we found ourselves at last at our desired haven, having been sixty-eight days in marching from Fort Smith to Fort Union. We encamped beside the first column, just outside the fort, and before my tent was pitched one of the officers brought a large bundle of letters to my ambulance; the lion's share I found belonged to Andrew and myself. With intense eagerness and impatience we tore them open, anxious, yet fearing to know of the events of the past three months. Thank God! All of our dear ones were well.

IV

Journey's End

Fort Union to Fort Stevens,
August–September, 1866

August 15

In one of my letters from Nelly I learned that my old friend Delia Thornton was married to Major Casey of the Fifth Infantry. Generals Garrard and Davidson, who called upon me last evening, told me that Major Casey and his wife were here—the regiment having arrived a few days ago with General Sykes in command. I rode over to see Delia at the Fifth Infantry Camp. I found her on crutches and looking very delicate. Her ambulance had been turned over the other side of the Raton Mountains, and she was badly hurt—had some ribs fractured and her back injured.[1] She was delighted to see me, and we had a long talk together about our mutual friends. I was very much pleased with her husband. He reminded me somewhat of Major Lockwood.

The Fifth Infantry expects to leave in a few days for Fort Sumner:[2] two companies of the Third go with them—Colonel DuBois and Major Tarleton. General Sykes wanted Andrew to go with them, but he has accepted the command of Fort Stevens, a post he is to establish in Colorado on the headwaters of the Arkansas. He received his orders last night and today moved to a separate camp with G Company and the companies of the Fifty-seventh Colored Infantry, which are to go with him. This will take us about 150 miles on the road back to the states and that much nearer our letters.

August 16

The new Fort Union has only been built about four years. It has very fine officers' quarters that have just been completed. They are built of adobe with zinc roofs and are very comfortable and nice looking.

Adobes are bricks made of mud and dried in the sun. I saw a large number of men engaged in making them. They were busy at a place where the mud had previously been dug up. They had wooden moulds just like a box with the top and bottom out. These they would lay on the ground, scoop up two or three double handfuls of the mud, and throw it in the mould, smooth it over with their hands, then pull up the mould and put it in a new place, leaving the brick standing. The sun dries these adobes in a few days, and then they are ready for use. All the houses in this country are built of them, and when they have a roof that does not leak they will last for years and years. But usually the little one-story houses here have a flat roof made of logs filled in with mud, and this affords but a poor protection against the rain.

I went over to the old fort about a mile distant to return the calls I had received from Captain Shoemaker's family. There, some of the old houses had quite a flower garden, which had sprung up from the mud on their roofs. Some of the old houses here have been torn down. I saw the house where George and Mary had lived, which was partly in ruins.[3]

August 18

The weather has been very cold since we arrived here, but today it has been more comfortable. I see by the letters and papers from the east that they have had excessively hot weather. With us, on the contrary, the weather has been charming; we only suffered from the heat two or three days on the whole trip, and that was when we were on the borders of the Staked Plain. We arrived here in the rainy season, as they have two in this country, and every day we are treated to a shower of rain. However, you can see it coming so long before it reaches you that it is not much annoyance.

Colonel Harwood has returned. Wandered back to Fort Smith nearly starved. Came from there here by stage.

Colonel Lane and his wife called this evening,[4] and also General Sykes. The latter is lieutenant colonel commanding the Fifth Infantry. General Carleton is in command of the district of New Mexico. Some dissatisfaction is felt at the way the Third Cavalry has been posted; it has been divided up into companies and sent around to posts commanded by infantry. Andrew is the only one of the line officers who will be in command of a post. Colonel Howe is sent with one company down to Fort Craig.[5]

August 20

This morning we left Fort Union after quite a sad parting from our brothers-in-arms, who came down in a body to our camp to say goodbye. The remainder leave in a day or two for their several posts. Colonel Howe escorted us from camp to General Carleton's headquarters, where Andrew reported before leaving. The old colonel expressed great regret at parting from us. He has been exceedingly kind and considerate to Andrew and me and has done everything in his power to add to our comfort, for which we feel very much indebted to him.

In consideration of Andrew's supposed feelings and my proximity to civilization, upon starting in the morning I abandoned my usual bizarre costume for a proper riding habit and a small cap. The consequence is the sun burnt my face nearly to a blister; indeed, it took the skin off both ears.

We marched about twenty miles.

August 22

During the day's march I went off the road about two miles with Andrew to see the Rayado Ranch, one of the most watered [?] in this country. It was formerly owned by Maxwell, but now belongs to Jesus Abrier, or, as his name sounds here, "Sussy Breer." [6] As I looked down upon this ranch, I seemed to see before me a picture of the olden times. In the centre was the fortified dwelling of the lord of the manor built around a spacious open square in which was grass and trees growing and surrounded by massive walls built, like the houses, of adobes. There was but one entrance to this court, through which we rode to look at the interior. Around this citadel were scattered smaller adobe houses, the homes of the Mexicans who worked on the ranch. The flat roofs with their gay flowers flaunting and the mamas and children who were seated upon them gazing at us gave an oriental appearance to the scene. Andrew said there must be a thousand Mexicans, little and big, at this ranch.

Here we had the old feudal system again. For refuge against a treacherous enemy these Mexicans had sought shelter under the walls of the fortified dwelling of this great landed proprietor. He gives them employment upon his ranch, owns the houses they live [in], and exercises over them the power of life and death, they say.

When Maxwell owned this ranch he was so threatened by the Indians that he got a six-pounder gun from the states and mounted it on top of one of the adobe houses. Shortly after, his ranch was invaded by five or six hundred Comanches, but as soon as they got within range he lit into them with grape, and Andrew says they have never stopped running yet. Indians are very much afraid of cannon, as they are rather beyond their comprehension.[7] We have two guns along with us for our new fort.

August 23

Saw a couple of Utah Indians today, a "buck" and a "squaw," who came riding along on a pair of Indian ponies. Their costume exceeded anything I have seen yet. The squaw had her hair divided into two tails, which were wound round and round with strings of small beads. Both her eyes and one of her cheeks were painted with vermilion. She was dressed like the buck in doeskin and one thing and another, and as she rode astride her horse it was hard to define her sex. Her horse's bridle was covered with little bells, which jingled as she rode along, and she had a very pretty saddle cloth woven with bright colors and with a tassel hanging from each corner.

The Navajos make beautiful saddle cloths, which they sell

from 10 to 150 dollars. Some of their blankets bring as much as 500 dollars. They are made by hand and so close that you can carry water in them.

August 24

On our march today we crossed again the Canadian River, which we have followed up almost from its mouth. Where we crossed it today it was no wider than the Willowbrook is at its mouth, and only a couple of feet deep.

Tomorrow we cross the Raton Mountains.[8] It seems strange enough to be as near the clouds as we are. They come sweeping down the sides of the mountains around us until they seem hardly fifty yards above us. Today the air was heavy and damp, and the clouds seem to settle right down upon the earth, shutting off the view around like a curtain. It still continues to rain some every day, but as the men got good "A" tents at Fort Union, we do not mind it much.

August 25

This morning we entered upon the pass of the Ratons. I had looked forward with much pleasure to this day's march, as the Raton Pass affords some of the finest scenery of the Rocky Mountains. Much to my disappointment, however, the fine, drizzling rain of last night continued this morning and shut out the view more completely than a fog. However, although the more distant mountains were hid from our view, yet as we passed through the narrow gorge we could see the mountains on each side towering above us in great wildness and beauty. A little stream runs through this mountain gorge which the road crosses fifty-seven times, they say. I began to count but gave up in despair after the tenth crossing—the jolting of the ambulance put the numbers out of my head.

We were delayed some time by meeting a wagon train hauling government supplies from Fort Riley [Kansas] to Fort Union. They were these immense wagons called out here "prairie schooners" and were hauled by five and six yoke of oxen.

We encamped about four miles from the summit of the

mountains in a little valley where there was fine grazing, having mached about eleven miles. To our great satisfaction in the afternoon the rain ceased and the sun broke out from the clouds. We have had a lovely evening, and there is every prospect of a charming day tomorrow for our further ascent of the mountains.

Andrew took the pups and walked up this valley with his rifle this afternoon and startled a black-tail deer two or three hundred yards from this camp. He followed him across the mountains for five or six miles but did not get a shot. He said it was astonishing to see the pups follow the deer's trail. He says he has raised a great many pups, but these are the most promising he has ever had. For the last six weeks they have been hunting everything they could find—they began with grasshoppers, which they would point at and then nibble, and Jack and Flos have each caught a field lark.

Andrew fetched me a bouquet from the top of the Rockies this evening. It consisted of blue harebells, ice larkspur, scarlet cypress, and two or three other flowers and was very pretty. Notwithstanding what I heard about the impossibility of raising flowers in New Mexico, I have seen a plenty of wild ones here.

August 26

We did not leave camp until late as, notwithstanding last evening's promise, the rain had again set in. It began with a thundershower about nine o'clock last night. A peal of thunder came rolling in among the mountaintops, gathering strength from its reverberations as it went on, and in a moment another well-known sound struck upon our ears—the heavy sound of horses' feet in the distance—a stampede. Andrew rushed from the tent crying, "Stand to horse!" and I followed him. The moon, whose dazzling brightness we had remarked early in the evening, lighted the summits of the tall mountains around us and shed her rays into the wild cañon where we were encamped. The moonlight, the white tents, the campfires, and the horses dashing madly through the valley, and the cries of the men who were trying to arrest them, made a wild and pictur-

esque scene—and even the fact of Zaidee being one of the
runaways could not hinder me from appreciating its beauty.
She was brought in this morning by some of the men who had
been out hunting the horses all night. Before we left camp all
the horses were recovered but two and two Indian ponies.
These Sergeant Armstrong went in search of, taking two days'
rations.

It rained when we started out, but I put on my waterproof
dress and took to the saddle, for the mountains were too beautiful to be hid by the top of an ambulance. Andrew paid me
the compliment of laughing at my costume. Besides my dress,
I wore my waterproof cloak, with the hood drawn over my
head, surmounted by one of Andrew's soft hats, the brim
turned down to shed the rain.

The shower held up when we reached the summit of the
mountain, and we had a view of the surrounding country
which was only limited by our powers of vision. At our right
the bleak rocky summit of Fisher's Peak reared itself above
our heads, and at the left the Spanish Peaks towered above
the clouds which hid also from our view the snowcapped top
of the Rocky Mountain range.[9] At our feet lay many a rocky
cañon and lovely valley, enameled with gay flowers, through
which we could trace our winding path for many miles. Upon
our descent we met with another clear mountain stream, whose
course we followed, crossing it innumerable times.

Formerly the passage of the Raton Mountains was somewhat perilous, as the road went through many a deep ravine
and along the edge of dangerous precipices, but within the last
two years a new road had been made (consisting principally
of countless little bridges) which is a great benefit to travelers
over the mountains.[10]

We encamped at night about seven miles from the top of
the mountains, our camp even more beautiful if possible than
that of last night. I think I never saw a bouquet of more ex-
quisite flowers than the one I gathered this evening upon the
side of the mountain. The blue harebell and scarlet cypress
flowers mingled with white, orange, and pink flowers, quite as
delicate, whose names were unknown to me.

August 27

Marched about ten miles and came to the little Mexican village of Trinidad upon the Purgatory,[11] a mountain stream which we found so swollen by the late rains as to be unfordable, so we retraced our steps and encamped about a mile from the river, where we have to wait patiently until it allows of our passing. A squadron of the Second Cavalry, who are escorting a paymaster to Santa Fe, are detained in like manner on the other side. There are two officers of the Third with it, one of them Lieutenant Thomas of G Company.

August 28

Rain fell last night, but this morning the weather was bright and beautiful, and the sunlight glistened upon the snow-capped tops of the Spanish Peaks, from which the clouds had at last lifted. The purity and transparency of the atmosphere —here I got stuck (Andrew suggests, "Oh, what a wonder! General Jackson, Hell and thunder.")—make the mountain-top seem very near, while the actual "Distance lends enchantment to the view, And clothes the mountain in its radiant hue."

August 29

Remained in camp. Armstrong returned with the horses.

August 30

As the river still continued unabated, Alexander started off early this morning with men and wagons to build a bridge, which he completed about four in the afternoon, and the command passed out of Purgatory and continued its march about five miles beyond the river, where we encamped for the night.

August 31

Marched twenty miles and encamped on the Apishapa River, where we are to remain until the locality of the post is decided by a board to consist of General Kit Carson, Colonel Enos, and Andrew, who are to meet next Monday for that purpose at Francisco's Ranch about twenty-five miles from here. Colonel Enos is camped on the other side of this river.

September 1

This morning Andrew started off with Colonel Enos and Colonel St. Vrain, an old settler in this country,[12] to explore the head of this creek. They went up ten or fifteen miles toward the Spanish Peaks and brought back a very favorable report of the land. Andrew said they found a fine place for a fort in a valley among the mountains through which this river flows. He said deer tracks were as thick there as if a flock of sheep had been driven over the country.

September 2

Andrew left at an early hour for Francisco's Ranch on the Cuchara. Today has seemed more like the Sabbath than any day since I left home. A profound quiet has rested upon the camp. The day warm and pleasant. The rainy season is probably over.

September 3

Another pleasant day. Remained quietly in camp.

September 4

Andrew returned this evening from Francisco's Ranch with the intelligence that the Cuchara River has been decided upon for our new post. He described it as a wild mountain country and made us all unhappy by dilating upon the breakfast he had enjoyed this morning of fine brook trout.

September 5

This morning we again started on our way congratulating ourselves that tomorrow's march would end our long journey. We made twenty miles and encamped on the Cuchara. A warm day.

September 6

This morning we started at daylight, as we had a long march of twenty-five miles before us to the head of the creek and wanted to get early in camp. Mr. Mulford took the troops along the river, while Andrew, who wished to get to camp in advance, got in the ambulance with me and went another road, which, though longer, was said to be better. However, in this case the first was last, for we lost our way, wandered over the prairie for some time, found ourselves after awhile on our back trail, and at last got into camp late in the afternoon, having taken a little march of fifty-five miles instead of twenty-five. We found Mr. Mulford greatly relieved at our arrival, as he was about starting off in search of us with twenty-five men, as he feared from our nonappearance the Utes had taken us.

All the command seemed in high spirits at the prospect of going permanently into camp. The site of our post could not be surpassed. Imagine a fine grassy plateau of seven or eight hundred acres skirted with timber and with the Cuchara, a beautiful trout stream, flowing through it. This is surrounded by an amphitheatre of mountains, in the center of which one of the Spanish Peaks rears its lofty head. From each side of this mountain extends a natural wall of rock bounding the valley on the right and left for two or three miles. These strata of rock are but five or six feet through and vary in height, being in some places two or three hundred feet high and in others broken down in gaps like a colossal wall partly in ruins. This singular phenomenon already gives the post the air of a fortress and adds also to its security in preventing flank movements.

September 7

We moved our camp this morning into a sheltered nook nearer the mountain, where we will remain until our permanent quarters are built. Busy all day in getting things to rights.

V

Campaigning in Colorado

Fort Stevens and Fort Garland,
September–October, 1866

September 19
Fort Stevens[1]

Yesterday Andrew received a note from General Sherman saying he would be at Fort Garland today, so Andrew went over to see him on business relating to the fort. This has been a wild, stormy evening, but I have been quite comfortable. I have a large hospital tent pitched in front of my small tent with a wide chimney and fireplace in which there is now a roaring fire, and I have been sitting in front of it writing home.

September 20

Have been busy all day fixing up my abode so that it will look pleasant on the return of my liege lord. Carroll received a dispatch from him this afternoon telling him to prepare for General Sherman's reception. So, although I have some few things to attend to myself, I had to go to work making bags for blank cartridges to give the general a salute.

About nine o'clock at night Andrew made his appearance with Colonel Audenried; they had ridden across the mountains from Garland that afternoon. My tent looked very nice when they came, and I was dressed in my best bib and tucker waiting for their coming.

September 21
Fort Stevens

Alexander and Audenried started off for a hunt this morning. We hear that Sherman has decided this post is to be abandoned, and this garrison is to move as soon as possible to Fort
Garland, which is at present garrisoned by Mexican volunteers
under the command of Kit Carson.[2] I am disgusted at the idea
of moving again, but after all it is about as well, as we hear
there are very comfortable quarters there all ready for us.

This evening we had quite a gay time. I invited Lizzie
Carroll and the officers in, and we had a candy pull. While the
candy was boiling we had a turn at "Shakespeare's Mental
Photographs," which afforded us a great deal of amusement.[3]
It seems curious enough to see Audenried out here, and I really
enjoy talking with him about Washington and our mutual
friends. He speaks in the highest terms of Marion, which,
under the circumstances, speaks well of both of them. [One]
only wonders "how she came to fancy Dutton." Poor Dutton,
he was ugly![4]

September 22

Have been looking around to see what preparation I could
make for the entertainment of the general, who is expected tonight or tomorrow morning. Housekeeping with a fly tent for a
kitchen is rather a sorry affair, however. Last evening, just at
dinner, the soup was overturned, and today I was deep in some
blanc mange when a sudden gust of wind blew all over me and
destroyed my morning's work. Also, one of my dinner plates
broke, leaving me with only five to entertain my guests. Nothing will be left for the great general directly but a tin plate.

September 23

A dark, foggy morning, and cold enough to make the bright
fire in our new chimney very pleasant. About eleven o'clock
small Jacob came galloping up to the tent with the information
that "the general is coming, sir." Whereupon Andrew fastened
on his sash and sabre and started out at the head of his company to meet the lieutenant general.

Such a dense fog obscured everything that we could not see the approach of the party, which was welcomed by a salute of fifteen guns. Soon General Sherman entered the tent and greeted me warmly. He was accompanied by Colonel Dayton, Captain McGinnis, his nephew Mr. Barclay (a boy of eighteen or nineteen), and a Captain Barlow. Colonel Audenried, his aide-de-camp, was here in advance of him.

There were two or three hospital tents pitched at the right of our tent with large fires blazing before them. These were the quarters we offered our guests. I had a larger table made the day before that would just seat eight comfortably. Soon after their arrival we had lunch in the mess tent. General Sherman occupied the seat of honor at my left, on the end of a trunk. I told him laughingly that the greatest luxury I was able to offer him here was what he had regretted upon leaving camp life for civilized regions—the privilege of throwing his coffee grounds on the floor. He took me at my word during his stay here, declaring that was really comfortable and that this was the only place where a man enjoyed true freedom. I reminded him that freedom's last retreat was always to the mountains.

I spent nearly all the afternoon tete-a-tete with him. He took great interest in pointing out to me the boundaries of the different departments in his command, showed me the new lines of railroads, and talked at length and most interestingly about this frontier land.[5] He asked me all about my trip across the plains and afterwards said to Andrew, "I declare, Alexander, your wife knows more about the country than you do"— an assertion which Andrew stoutly denied, saying there was no one who had ever traveled through this country that knew more about it than he.

We had dinner about six o'clock. I had the table brought in this tent, where it was warm and cheerful. It is the fashion after entertaining great men to publish your bill of fare, so I will note mine here. First course, beef vegetable soup; second, saddle of mutton with jelly, green peas, kirshaw squash, cabbage, and beets; third, soft custard, blanc mange with cream and sugar, and coffee. Everything was cooked to perfection, and the general declared he had not tasted so fine a saddle of mutton since he left Saint Louis and said it was the king of dishes. I must say they all ate with a good appetite, and our chief honored the mutton so far as to return to it a third time.

Our dinner was seasoned with a great deal of spicy conversation, stories of camp and field which always abound when old soldiers get together. Andrew told two or three anecdotes at Sherman's expense, which the latter seemed to enjoy hugely. In the evening all the officers dropped in, and Mrs. Carroll came too, and was greeted very kindly by Sherman. Sherman and Andrew kept the conversation afloat with many amusing and interesting reminiscences, which greatly edified the surrounding company. I sat in a corner on a trunk with Audenried, and we talked together of our mutual friends and of our experience in married life.

In the evening, after all had left, I told Andrew of a remark Audenried had made that he did not let his wife write or give her picture to any gentleman, and [he] in return exercised the same restraint in regard to ladies. Andrew thought it was the most shocking arrangement he had ever heard, and we talked for a long time about the strange folly of jealousy. Andrew got really eloquent on the subject, said he thought it the greatest indelicacy for a man to imagine his wife could commit an indecorum in writing or giving her picture to anyone she chose.

September 24

After breakfast this morning General Sherman and party took their leave. They were accompanied for four or five miles by a mounted escort with drawn sabres—Lieutenants Thomas and Mulford and Andrew and myself—riding at a full gallop. I enjoyed the ride although it was a rather stormy morning. General Sherman was very kind at parting, thanked us for our attentions, said he never should forget me or his visit to the Spanish Peaks, and hoped I would not fail to call upon him if he could ever be of service to me.[6]

September 27

Today we received letters from home, the first we have had in a month. Andrew heard from Midge and from Apo— the latter is at Silver Springs and writes that she is going to send Jim to us for a year on account of his health, which is very delicate. As soon as she returns to Saint Louis she will send him out by Andrew, who is home on a furlough.[7]

I had also letters from Nelly and Emily giving full accounts of a dinner the Auburn people gave the President and his party in our grove. Grant and Farragut and the President being there made it very interesting for all our people, and Joe Fullerton made his appearance there at the same time.[8]

But I have thought very little of this in comparison with the information conveyed to me in a passing remark of Nelly's that *Lily is engaged.* Who to I cannot imagine, unless it is to young Tremaine, who they have mentioned as being there this summer and speak very highly of. I cannot express here how deeply this intelligence has affected me. I am anxious, very, to know who is the fortunate man, and yet it seems as if no one was good enough or clever enough for our young, lovely, beautiful Lily. I have imagined her for many a year yet the light of the household at Willowbrook, and now as Andrew says she is already beginning to flutter her wings. He has been looking rather *triste* as we talked of it this evening and has been singing to himself:

> "Coo-o, says the little dove
> Coo-o-o, says she
> And away they flew from the old oak tree."

September 29

We had a large mail from home last night giving us full particulars of Lily's fiancé. It is as I imagined—Grenville Tremaine, and from all accounts he must be, as they say, "one in a thousand." I wrote tonight to mother and Lily at length. I have been very much moved at learning of this affair of such deep importance to my little sister. Andrew shakes his head about it, on account of the long engagement which is to ensue and the "no spondulix," as he says. He thinks one in the family is enough to make a bad match. However, I do not share his horror of long engagements and think in this case it will be a good thing.[9]

October 1

Information came this morning from Trinidad that a large body of Indians had encamped there and were making a disturbance with the inhabitants, who begged the colonel to come over. So Andrew started off with the whole of G Company and Lieutenants Thomas and Mulford. I accompanied him five miles on the way and then returned to camp. It looked so lonesome in my quarters that I sent and invited Mr. Shoemaker to dinner. He spent the evening with me, and we had quite a sociable time.

October 2

This is a charming, bright day, as indeed all this last week has been. I have been quite distressed all day about Fly and Comet, our new greyhound pups, who are so sick with the distemper that they will not eat a mouthful, and I am afraid they are going to die.

October 4

This morning we received a dispatch by a Mexican from Andrew. He had a severe skirmish with the Indians, killed thirteen, and lost one man killed and two wounded. He heard when at Trinidad that they were attacking a ranch five miles distant, so he put his horses to the gallop and soon came up to them. He wrote that he had whipped them handsomely when his ammunition gave out, and the Indians retreated to the mountains, two or three only of them following him, endeavoring to recover the bodies of their dead, which Andrew carried off. He sent for more carbines and ammunition, as there was a large body of citizens helping him; he informed Kit Carson and Maxwell by courier of the state of affairs, and told Mr. Carroll to move our camp down onto the plain to consolidate it as much as possible and throw up breastworks.

This letter put the camp into quite a state of commotion.

Everyone was at once busy packing up and preparing to move. I was hard at work till noon packing up my china, my books, and my seven trunks. Mr. Carroll suggested that I should take Lizzie and go over to Garland, but I told him I preferred remaining in camp to trusting myself with a Negro guard across the mountains. I took the precaution, however, to have my revolver newly loaded and capped, and with this and the pups for company I am alone in my tent tonight. Outside I hear the Negro guard challenging a passerby, "Who goes da?" and the answer is "A friend."

October 6

We were eating lunch together today, and talking about the Indians, when suddenly we heard a yell and a couple of shots fired and saw a body of mounted men dashing upon our herd of horses about a thousand yards off on the plain. I exclaimed, "There they are!" and we all sprang from the table, our hearts in our mouths. "To arms!" someone yelled without waiting for a bugle, and in a moment our camp was in a state of excitement, one buckling on his pistol, another loading his gun, some crying for caps, some for cartridges, while others were saddling up. In an incredibly short time, Captain Stewart, at the head of his darkies, had started after our large cattle herd that the Indians were making for. Our horses were already safe. Livingstone was the only one with them, as the rest of the herders had gone to dinner. When he caught sight of the Indians he galloped round the horses and started them into camp; they rushed as usual to the picket line, and he fell, shot in the shoulder with an arrow.

When the alarm was first given I sprang to my tent and buckled on my revolver that was lying ready loaded on the table. My next thought was for Lizzie Carroll, whose husband was at that moment busy loading our two cannon. I called her and, casting my eye around, selected a small tent which was surrounded on two sides by boxes and flour sacks as the safest position in case our camp should be attacked. I put her in this tent and then looked round for Zaidee, and was greatly relieved when I saw the faithful Errickson leading her in. I had her fastened right near this tent, and then, as the dogs were all at my feet, I felt as if I had my family around me and had leisure to watch operations.

There were only fifteen or twenty Indians in the party that was endeavoring to stampede and carry off our horses. Reports were brought in that there were from sixty to one hundred in the timber beyond the plateau. This may be, but it is certain that there were not more than twenty visible at any time. They skirmished around camp for some time, keeping out of rifle range, and then went off towards Francisco's ranch, about five miles below us, where they carried off twenty horses. This was the last we saw of them, but for the rest of the day we were busy enough preparing for another visit and completing our breastworks.

I spent the afternoon in the hospital with Livingstone, whom I do not think dangerously wounded. The doctor is at Trinidad attending to the men who were shot in the fight there, so McCallum is the only one left to look after this man, and as he is not often sober, I did not dare to leave him alone with the patient. Outside I heard the darkies chattering like so many magpies, as they were busily engaged throwing up a small earthwork. "O! Lor me!" said one, "How I wish de kernel had been yere. He'd got those black debels." "I'd like to go fer dem," said another. And several came to me in the evening to know, "When de kernel coming back?"

Soon after dark the camp was aroused by the rapid firing of the pickets, and the alarm was given. A body of the troops were said to be moving up the valley. They proved, however, to be the absent scouting party, who, after having marched sixty miles that day across the mountains in pursuit of the Utes, found their friends more dangerous than their foes. The darkies had been fully aroused to the necessity of vigilance and fired as they had been ordered without challenging. It was not until the newcomers had replied satisfactorily to their brilliant question, "How long hab you bin gone?" that they were allowed to come into camp.

Andrew was accompanied with about seventy-five citizens from the Pickets mine who had volunteered to go with him in this pursuit of the Indians. They had followed close upon their trail for the last three days but had not come up with them since their fight. We could see their signal fires burning brilliantly upon the side of a mountain about seven miles off, and the determination was to "go for them" early in the morning.

Andrew gave me an account of his proceedings at Trinidad. The day before the fight he had a council at which a large number of the Indians and inhabitants were assembled. Andrew asked Keneatze, the chief of the Utes,[10] what reason he gave for coming and destroying the crops of these people and carrying off their stock, to which he promptly replied, "That the land belonged to him, and when his children were hungry he would come and take food for them." Throughout the "pow-wow" the chief and the Indians displayed a bad spirit. Andrew told Keneatze to come back early the next morning and he would talk with him. But the chief said he would not come, at which Andrew rose up from his chair and, walking across to Keneatze, shook his finger in his face and said to the interpreter, "You tell this old scoundrel that if he does not meet me tomorrow morning, I'm mad," and then stalked out of the room, leaving the Indians astonished and the Mexicans aghast, for no one had ever dared to talk this way to the Indians before.

The next morning Keneatze did not make his appearance, and Andrew sent a Mexican over posthaste to tell him he must come over and see him or he and his band must leave the country. While he was gone the people asked Andrew what he would do if Keneatze would not come, to which Andrew quietly replied he would fight him. This reply astonished them, as Andrew only had sixty men and there were several hundred Indians, but many of the old mountaineers went off to get their rifles ready. The courier came back at a full run, saying Keneatze wanted to fight and was attacking a ranch about five miles up the river. At which Andrew had "boots and saddles" sounded and took the gallop and [fell] upon the

Indians who expected to commit their havoc and get off as usual before the approach of the troops.

There were about two hundred warriors drawn up to meet them, which Andrew attacked with his sixty men and after a sharp skirmish whipped them thoroughly. He could not pursue them though, as his ammunition was exhausted, as his men only had twenty rounds apiece. The Indians left thirteen dead upon the field and had a number wounded. We had one man and three horses killed and two men and two horses wounded. The field presented a curious view—it was strewed with bows and arrows, shields, and pieces of buffalo skins. I had brought to me as trophies the eagle off Keneatze's hat, which he lost in the fight, and an arrow which poor Brickson received. The inhabitants hereabouts say that they never knew of these Utes being so badly beaten before. Those that were here today belonged to the same band.[11]

October 7

This morning, as soon as possible, Andrew started off again in hot pursuit of the Utes. He took with him G Company, Lieutenants Thomas and Mulford, and the seventy-five volunteers from Trinidad. These were divided into two companies, Mexicans and Americans, and were a motley crew indeed. Many of them were mounted on mules Andrew furnished them, others rode little ponies, and they were armed with everything from a pistol to a long rifle and a musket with a bayonet on the end. At a distance it would be impossible to tell them from the Utes themselves, for most of them were dressed in buckskin shirt and leggings and had a white striped blanket over their shoulders. They seemed to be in high spirits and were laughing and shouting in a very unmilitary way. They all seemed to have taken an immense liking to Andrew and to feel unbounded confidence in him. Andrew expects to be gone from five to seven days and intends to finish up the Ute nation or his horses before he stops. Meantime we are to move to Garland.

Last night we had another slight alarm, but it proved to be a cow that the darkies challenged. We hear that the In-

dians yesterday morning killed two men at Badito and carried
off a woman and four children.[12] They drove off all the stock
also. I expect Andrew will catch up with them today.

I have just been in to see Willis, the man who was shot at
Trinidad. (Arly, who was wounded with an arrow, was not
much hurt.) This poor fellow will probably lose his leg. He
is suffering very much. He told me that he surely thought
the colonel would be killed, for they were all shooting at him.
Willis said the ball that hit him was aimed at the colonel (Andrew had told me the same thing before) and said he was glad
he was shot and not the colonel. [The Indians] all knew Andrew was the chief, as they saw him at the council, and as
he was the only one mounted during the fight they easily
picked him out. But he has thus far been preserved from "the
arrow that flieth by day."[13]

October 11
Fort Garland[14]

We left Fort Stevens Tuesday the 9th and had a tiresome
trip across the mountains. The roads were frightful, and as
we traveled with the train we went horribly slow. The
wounded men who were with us suffered very much from
traveling, and I agonized a good deal over them. At last today
at noon my patience became utterly exhausted, and I an-
nounced to Mr. Carroll my intention of pushing on to Fort
Garland with Dr. Lee and the wounded men. I took with me
about a dozen armed men, and Mrs. Carroll went with us.

After I had traveled about a mile, my ambulance broke
down. I was not in it, fortunately, and we lashed a pole under
the axletree and dragged it along. Further on I met a detachment of Mexican Cavalry going to Garland. I sent word by
them to Alexander that I was on my way and to come and meet
me. So about sunset, when we were within four miles of
Garland, Andrew made his appearance in General Carson's
carriage, and very glad I was to see him after his ten days'
scout.

I had abandoned my baggage when I hurried on and had
nothing with me except the inevitable pups. So we took advan-

tage of General Carson's hospitality and took supper and spent the night with him.

October 12

Andrew was sick today with a severe cold, so I dined alone with old Kit Carson. He is a most interesting, original old fellow. Today I drew him out, and he told me a great many interesting things about the Pueblos.[15] At Taos, the Montezuma fires are still burning as they have been for hundreds of years, without being ever extinguished. He says at the Pueblo village near Taos every morning at sunrise all the Indians go up on top of their houses and look towards the rising sun to see if Montezuma has yet appeared, for they have a legend that he will come again some day at the sunrising.[16]

He told me also of a night he spent, years ago, in Keneatze's camp and how till near the small hours the old chief discoursed to him, between intervals of smoking, of the future country of the Indians. They would all gradually disappear from this land, he said, but would assemble, immortal, in another world. In that country there would be some Mexicans, but no white people, *not one*. All the game which the Indians had killed from the earliest periods of time would there reappear; the Indians who had died natural deaths would wear the same appearance they formerly did on earth, but the warriors who had fallen in battle would be pale and bloody. And after awhile, when all the Indians had been gathered into that other country, they would then come again to this world and dwell here supreme forever.[17]

October 13

This morning I went out with Kit Carson to visit the Indian encampment about five miles out. I rode Zay, and she never appeared fitter. General Carson declared she was the finest animal he had ever seen.[18]

When we were out about halfway, we were met by Oulay and half a dozen of his men. He is the finest Indian I have seen yet, good looking, dignified, and from all I can learn, honest and reliable. He was not engaged in the late dis-

turbance. He carried off his band of Utes and warned the
people of the Huerfano of the coming of the hostile Indians.
He acted throughout in a very praiseworthy manner, and old
Kit says, "I shall always treat Oulay just like a white man,
for he is a good Injun."[19]

Oulay and his party escorted us out to their camp, and
as I looked behind me as we galloped on I imagined the wonder and curiosity our escort would have excited in Central
Park, for instance. Immediately behind us were some hunters
clad in buckskin shirt and trousers, fringed and embroidered,
then came the Indians whooping to their ponies as they went,
dressed in buckskin, bright blankets, gay beads, and feathers,
their bows and arrows slung on their backs behind, encased
in horseskin, and their rifles in front.

When we got to their village we found about a thousand
wild Indians encamped there. They did not have skin wigwams
like the Prairie Indians, but their wigwams were of drilling
and looked like Sibley tents (which in fact were copied from
these wigwams). In front of the warriors' tents were stuck up
their spears, ornamented with eagles' feathers and with their
painted shields and head ornaments of feathers hanging to
them.[20]

We went to Oulay's tent, and he politely asked me in, but
I declined to get down from my horse. Then his squaw (the
finest-looking Indian woman I have seen) brought me a cup of
water, which I accepted. A crowd of Indians gathered round
and gazed at me steadily and immovably. Many of them had
red blankets, which they seemed to wear in the Mexican
fashion, over their heads and drawn round over their mouths.
We rode around the camp and passed one wigwam where
somebody was sick and where they were making medicine. The
tent was filled with Indians, principally squaws and papooses;
they sat round in a circle and droned a low, chanting song.

It was pleasant to see the effect old Kit's appearance had
on these savages. Instead of the sullen, stolid appearance I
had always noticed on them before, their faces brightened with
smiles as they held out their hands to him with the salutation,

"Como le va?" or the Indian, "Hough!" He shook hands with one old squaw who seemed right pleased to be noticed. He told me when he went on his last campaign against the Navajos with his regiment, he was accompanied by fifty Utes, and this old squaw went with them all the way.[21]

October 20

Went out for a ride on Zay. She was in gay spirits; I could hardly hold her. Kit Carson pointed out the range of mountains in the distance over which Frémont traveled and the peaks where his party fell to eating one another in their frenzy from the want of food. He was away at the time, after supplies, but when he returned he saw fragments of their frightful repast.[22]

October 21   Sunday

I spent a good deal of the morning at the hospital reading to Willis and Livingstone. I go to see them most every day. Poor fellows, they both suffer very much, especially Willis. They always seemed right glad to see me.

We have very comfortable quarters here, though we are rather cramped, as we have given Mr. and Mrs. Carroll one of our rooms and have to live in one room and eat in the kitchen. Mr. Carroll has gone over to Trinidad to be gone several days, and his small wife is in a frightful state of loneliness during his absence. Andrew read me a sermon this afternoon, and I had her in.

October 22

General Carson left today for Maxwell's ranch with Keneatze and his band, which have been ordered to go back there.[23] He took his family down to Taos for the winter and has turned over his house to us. I went to the door and saw the party start. Keneatze and two other chiefs were in an ambulance. They all looked glum. One of the chiefs had a tomahawk in his hands, the first I have seen. It was a good deal ornamented with brass and silver.

October 24

We have had quite an interesting affair today—the distribution of presents to the Utes. They were all assembled in an area back of our quarters, seated on the ground in a large circle, two deep. The bucks [sat] on one side, the squaws and their young ones on the opposite. The great warriors sat by themselves and were distinguished by the immense appendages they wore on their heads, a succession of silver plates fastened together and hanging from the back of their heads to the ground. I saw one who instead of silver plates had six feet of tin pastry pans hanging from his "que" behind. The squaws wear their hair short usually, but their lords wear theirs as long as possible and generally divided into two tails, which are braided and covered with bits of worsted and strings of beads or with strips of beaver skin. I saw one Indian about five feet high who had his hair braided in a tail behind which hung down to his feet. Andrew said he probably had horse hair braided in with it.

The presents were all spread out in the midst of the circle and consisted of bales of blankets, red scarfs and handkerchiefs, tobacco, rice, sugar, shades [parasols], saws, awls, shirts, drilling, tin pans, etc. Before the distribution began, Oulay, the head chief, stood up and harangued the circle in Indian, telling them to keep quiet and behave themselves decently while they were receiving their presents. He was dressed very handsomely, in real Indian style. His leggings and hunting coat were richly and beautifully embroidered with beads, he had very small feet, and his moccasins fitted him perfectly. His hands, too, were small and well shaped. Around him he had a bright Navajo blanket, and he stood and walked around with the stateliness of one of Cooper's Indians.[24]

The presents were distributed by the Indian agents and by several chiefs. All seemed in great good humor and very well pleased with the occasion. The last thing distributed was the sugar. The barrels had been broken and it lay in a great pile in the middle. Of this they decided to make a grand game of "grab," and it was great sport to see the Indians and squaws rushing for it. It came near ending in a general fight;

knives were drawn and axe handles brandished, but the
chiefs went in and stopped it at once, and finally the curious
crowd departed, many of their ponies heavily laden with
squaws, papooses, and plunder.

October 26

All day I have been busily engaged in moving over to
General Carson's quarters, which he turned over to us. We
got comfortably established by night, and about sunset the
mail from Santa Fe brought us orders to go to Fort Union.
We were somewhat disgusted at first, for we are comfortably
settled for the winter, but after talking the matter over together, we decided it was not worthwhile to fret over anything, but began to enumerate the advantages of the new post
with its mail three times a week, etc.

A few days ago Andrew received the appointment of
major, Ninth Colored Cavalry, with orders to report immediately to New Orleans. He will not go across the plains
this winter, however, and has sent on to [General] Comstock his acceptance and nonacceptance—the latter to be sent
in in case Comstock cannot get his orders changed so that we
can remain here till spring. These new colored regiments are
to be splendidly officered. In the Ninth the colonel is Edward
Hatch, the lieutenant colonel Wesley Merritt, and the three
majors, Andrew, Sandy Forsyth, and a Major Wade, formerly
of the Sixth Cavalry.[25]

VI

Garrison Duty in New Mexico

Fort Garland to Forts Union, Bascom, and Sumner,
October, 1866–January, 1867

October 30
Fort Garland

This morning we packed up all our worldly goods for about the hundredth time and started them off for Fort Union. Lieutenant Mulford started in command of the column. We are not going to camp out but will ride ahead in the ambulance and wait over at the different Mexican towns for the train to catch up with us.

I secured quite a valuable trophy a few days ago—an Indian war shield. When I was at the Ute encampment I saw several [and] General Carson told me the Indians valued them very highly and that a shield and head gear were worth a good horse. The old chief who brought this to me was called Shawynoa.[1] He charged fifty dollars for the shield, but after some conversation in signs, and in what little Spanish I had picked up, he decided to let me have the "atap" for twenty dollars and two red blankets. It was an uncommonly handsome one, profusely ornamented with scarlet cloth and eagles' feathers, and had a fine cover of white buckskin. A few days ago I bought a bow and six arrows of him. The bow is very handsome, and the arrows are "war arrows" painted and marked with deep lines along their length.

Dr. Kugler of this post brought me in yesterday a bundle of arrows as a present. There were two or three different kinds, among them half a dozen Apache arrows that were poisoned.

I don't much think we shall remain at Union more than three or four weeks, as there is no need for cavalry there. I should be very glad to go to Maxwell's ranch, but otherwise I prefer remaining quietly at Fort Union until spring.

November 2
San Fernando de Taos[2]

We left Garland day before yesterday and spent that night at Costilla at Mr. Myers' house who entertained us very hospitably. Yesterday we marched forty-five miles over a very hilly country and spent last night at Arroyo Honda, twelve miles from Taos, at the house of Monsieur LeBlanc.[3] We found our host to be a most interesting and historical character. He is an old mountaineer and has been forty-six years in this country. He, with two companions, rescued the survivors of Frémont's exploring expedition from their living grave in the Sierra Nevada.

None of these mountain men seem to have a very high opinion of Frémont's abilities. LeBlanc told us that Frémont had Bill Williams for a guide and that he knew all those mountains as well as he knew the rooms in his own house. Bill Williams urged Frémont not to go into those mountains, for he said it was too late in the season and they would be snowed in, but Frémont insisted upon going. He wanted to look for a place to build a railroad to California, LeBlanc added.

In one night 150 mules were killed by the cold, and then Bill Williams urged them all to stop there and go to work and dry this mule meat, for they would be obliged to winter there now and this would keep them from starving. But Frémont would not hear of this and determined to push on afoot. He only succeeded, however, in getting a few miles, and then began their life of horrid privation. Frémont did not dare to remain with his command lest they should kill him, but he and Alick Gordon kept always sixteen or twenty miles ahead. These two at length came across two or three Utes who had a wagon and had been trapping. They rescued Frémont and his companion and carried them down the country. The first house they came to was the one in which LeBlanc lived: at that time there were only two or three shanties at Rio Honda. Frémont told his story to LeBlanc, and he immediately started off that day with two companions and provisions in search of the lost ones. The first person he met was old Bill Williams, whom he had long known, and as soon as Bill saw him he lifted up his gun to shoot him, but LeBlanc cried out to him and Bill recognized him. He had mistaken him for one of the party coming to murder him.

LeBlanc went on further and picked up parties of three or four—they did not dare to remain together, for to satisfy their frightful hunger the strong were killing the weak. Some of them were cooking when LeBlanc appeared and immediately threw out the contents of the kettles into the snow, but he told me he found there the remains of human limbs, hands, etc. All of the party had perished but fifteen or sixteen, and they could not have survived more than three or four days longer.

They would have killed themselves with excessive eating, but LeBlanc would only give them corn meal gruel, which he fed them with every two or three hours for days, until they gradually regained strength. They had been snowed up in the mountains for two months.[4]

LeBlanc had a great many interesting incidents to tell us of his life in the Rocky Mountains. During the insurrection in Taos in '48, when Governor Bent was killed, he and nine other mountaineers were besieged in a distillery by the Pueblos and Mexicans for three days and nights. Their assailants finally succeeded in setting fire to the house, and the little garrison were obliged to cut their way out through hundreds of the enemy. Only three of the ten succeeded in making their escape—LeBlanc was one of them—the rest were killed.[5]

We bade adieu to the old mountaineer this morning and came on to Taos, the second town of importance in the territory. As we approached the town, situated in a well-watered valley and skirted by high mountains, I was struck with the resemblance it bore to the pictures one sees of towns in Palestine. It was surrounded apparently by a thick wall. The streets were narrow, the houses the usual adobe structures, one story high, and the roofs flat and affording a place of resort to women and children, many of whom were gazing [at] us from the housetops, all but their eyes muffled up from view in true oriental fashion. In the centre of the town is a large plaza surrounded by nice-looking stores—evidence of American enterprise. Several streets led out from this. All the houses are built in the form of a square around an open courtyard called a plaza, into which each room usually opens. Thus, each house is a little castle, as the outer wall of the square has no windows or opening except the entrance.

Andrew had a letter to a Mr. Scheurich at Taos; we found the gentleman, and he gave us a cordial welcome. He is a German, has been in this country fifteen or sixteen years, and has married a daughter of old Governor Bent, an exceedingly pretty, graceful woman who speaks English very nicely, though she is rather timid about [it]. They have been married a year and a half and have a very handsome baby six months old, whom they call Alice. The little creature already wears earrings, and her mother showed me three or four tiny pair— the baby's property. Mr. Scheurich laughingly said, "In this country the first thing is get the baby baptized, then pierce its ears."

This house is very comfortable and well furnished. I have a very nice room, carpeted, papered, and with a French bedstead, etc., in it. The parlour, though, has a Mexican aspect; it has a good cottage piano (the first I have seen in this country), but the remainder of the furniture consists of cushions arranged around the room upon which everyone reclines. The scene this evening was heightened by the presence of Señora Teresina Scheurich and a visitor of hers who each regaled themselves with a "cigaretto" as they chatted together in a corner of the room.[6]

November 3
Taos

This is the second anniversary of our wedding day, and we celebrated it this morning by an excursion to the village of the Pueblo Indians about three miles from town. We had a most interesting visit there. These Indians derive their name from their living altogether in a "pueblo," the Spanish for town.

As we approached their village, it presented all the appearance of the ruins of an old castle, and the nearer we got, the stranger it looked. There were about fifteen hundred Pueblos living here in two villages a few hundred yards apart and separated by a beautiful stream of water which flowed down from the mountains close by. Both of these piles presented an extraordinary appearance. They were alike built of adobe, smoothly plastered outside, and each covering about two acres of ground. There was no entrance at the first story, except by means of ladders which led up to the second story. There were six or eight of these stories, irregularly built and each one smaller than the other, the highest consisting of only two or three rooms. These were all entered by ladders on the outside, and the rooms (or houses) connected with others below by inside ladders. These houses were kept very clean, outside and in, and Andrew and I explored one thoroughly, somewhat at the risk of our necks, for their ladders were perfectly perpendicular. The edifice was covered with high, narrow chimneys topped with earthenware pots which in the distance looked like pinnacles.[7]

When we arrived at the settlement we found all the Indians of both villages busily engaged in cleaning up the place. Some were sweeping the ground, others carrying off the dirt in their blankets, and the rest burning up the stubble. They were having a general policing before Sunday—a sight you never see in a Mexican town—and indeed the condition of the premises would have done credit to a post and put Fort Garland to shame.

Many of the children were as naked as they came into the world, and a number of little girls who followed us around had little babies tied on their backs in blankets. One little fellow was fast asleep, and another, when I nodded my head at him, laughed like a white baby.

We saw the ruins of their old church, which was nearly destroyed by Price during the insurrection of the Pueblos and

Mexicans in '47. They would never use it again, but built a new church, which we visited. The church was built of adobe, long and rather narrow. The altar was adorned with a large wooden image of the Virgin, dressed in tinsel, and a number of oil paintings coarsely executed. The most conspicuous we decided must be meant for Cortez and was immediately over the Virgin. It represented a caballero, mounted on a fiery horse and bearing a large tricolored flag—red, white, and green with a cross in the field. At the horseman's feet were several men of a diminutive size lying prostrate. There was a large picture of the Virgin, and peeping out from behind the skirt of her dress was a large representation of the sun. There was another very old picture of the Virgin painted on a buckskin, several feet long. It had probably been rescued from the old church.[8]

These Pueblos are probably some of the converts of the old Spaniards. They are very strict Catholics, I hear, and very rigid in their penitence and observances. Nevertheless, they still cling to some of their old superstitions. The fires of Montezuma have been kept continually burning here for hundreds of years. I visited two of these "estoffes." Above they presented the appearance of a mound with an opening in the centre. Through this I descended into the interior by means of a steep ladder. I found myself in a dome-shaped room only lighted from the opening in the top. In the centre of the floor was a square opening of hard adobe, having at one side a triangular wall three feet high. This opening was filled with white ashes—several feet deep, I have heard. Here the fires had become extinct.

We asked the Indian who accompanied us where were the estoffes where the fires were continually burning, but he denied that there was any such place. After some time, though, just as we were going away, Mr. Scheurich persuaded him to show us the place, and we entered another estoffe which they called "La Casa de Montezuma." Inside it appeared like the other except there were some faggots and straw in the interior; and by the square opening were several sheepskins where we were told an old man and two boys always slept at night to guard the fire. The opening was filled with white ashes, very hot, however. I, not yet content, took a wooden paddle lying near and, clearing off the white ashes, brought to our view burning hot and bright the sacred fires of Montezuma. I put some of the ashes in my handkerchief and brought [them] away with me for a souvenir.[9]

Within a few miles of Taos there are very extensive ruins of a city which once contained probably fifty thousand inhabitants. Nothing is left now but the stone foundations of the houses, which are sufficient, however, to indicate the different rooms and houses and streets. These ruins extend over several miles. I think there is no tradition extant with reference to the former inhabitants.[10]

November 4

Left Taos this morning to continue our journey. Our friends seemed to regret our leaving, and Señora Teresina gave me a little ring at parting. Camped at night with the command. Rather cold weather, too, to camp in the "Cañon de Taos."

November 5

Made a good march today and camped at Guadalupita twenty-five miles from Union. Andrew and I spent the night at a Mexican ranch and had an amusing time trying to talk Spanish with the ranchero and his wife. The man asked us if we had a baby, and when we replied in the negative, he said quite plaintively, "Me, my wife matrimonio ocho annos (eight years) and no baby!" and shook his head mournfully.

The señora showed me her jewelry during the evening, as is the custom of the country. She had a handsome necklace and earrings, Mexican work (which her husband informed me he paid 180 dollars for), and a curious girdle of solid silver set with colored stones of some sort. In return I showed her my trinkets, as I happened to have my jewel box along with me.

November 6

Arrived about noon today at Union. Found quarters awaiting us in Colonel Marshall's house. There was no comfortable place for the Carrolls, so we let them have one of our rooms.[11] Mrs. Marshall is a very pretty young woman, a daughter of Mr. Errickson, a banker of Rochester. I am very pleasantly impressed with her. Her husband is very much of an invalid, the result of wounds received during the war. Mrs. Marshall and Mrs. Bankhead are the only ladies at the post.

November 11

Had a visit from old Kit today. He had just come from Maxwell's, where he has been settling Keneatze's band. He said he had deposed Keneatze from his position and made Unketathe the principal chief.[12] He says Keneatze and some of his "young men" have just started off on a plundering expedition west of the Rio Grande against the Navajos.

[Kit] expressed a great deal of regret that he had not been at Taos when we visited there and gave me some interesting details respecting the Pueblo Indians there. He said many of their dances were very curious and described one called the Elk Dance in which the Indians dressed themselves up with the horns of various wild animals on their heads while young boys were provided with bows and arrows of straw with which they shot at the masquers as they danced around in a circle.[13] He told me also in regard to the sacred fires that the priests said (and they should know, if anyone, said old Kit) that children were still sacrified in these estoffes once a year. "I don't know whether it is true, but that is what the priests say."[14]

Old Kit also told me of the Moqui villages two or three hundred miles west of the Rio Grande which he had often visited.[15] These seven villages are built on high buttes connected by a narrow ledge of rock. The only way of approaching them is by artificial steps or holes cut into the solid rock, by which you ascend from the plain several hundred feet. These Indians made their homes in these inaccessible buttes as a protection from other tribes. Kit says that a pathway ten or twelve inches deep has been worn in the solid rock that connects the different buttes by the Indians passing from one village to another. These Moqui Indians still continue the worship of fire and have their estoffes of the same dome-like shape excavated in the living rock. How they ever made them he could not think. It is in these estoffes the Indians hold all their solemn councils, one of their number remaining above at the entrance to keep watch.

General Carson seemed much surprised to see my war shield [and] said they were very hard to get and that Chaveneau [Shawynoa] must have wanted money badly.

November 20

A lovely warm day. Went riding with Andrew and Mr. Mulford, started a wolf, and had an exciting chase after it. Maida ran well, but the wolf had too much the start of us and reached its covert in safety. The country around here is very fine for running wolves, as it is smooth and not under-mined by prairie dogs.

November 22

Andrew had a successful wolfhunt today and brought home a fine skin. Mai distinguished herself [and] took hold of the wolf with good pluck, but Andrew finally killed it with his pistol. Running wolves and foxes is the only amusement one has here, as there is no game around, and I am sorry to say the frequent windstorms and dust make any outdoor exercise almost impracticable.

November 24

Quite a large party arrived from the states today, some officers of the Fifth Infantry, a number of the Third Cavalry, and the chaplain for this post, Mr. Morte, his wife, and two daughters. We opened our house on the occasion and took in Captain Tilford, wife and baby and nurse, and his sister-in-law, Miss Dean. We gave them our bedroom and dining room and slept in the parlour ourselves, as we only have three rooms and a kitchen. Mrs. Tilford has a most lovely little girl three years old called Nina, a beautiful little fairy. Besides these, Captain Cressy, Captain Kemble, Captain McMullen, and Mr. Mulford take their meals with us, so we have quite a houseful.

November 29

Emily's birthday— "Sweet and twenty." It was also Thanksgiving Day, and I had quite a dinner party. Besides my large family I had the chaplain and his family, Mrs. Whiting, and Captain Inman. We had a very successful dinner and all seemed to enjoy themselves. My thoughts during the day were often with my family of a year ago, and I sighed for Croquet Cottage and *my boys*.

December 1

Andrew received today a copy of an order from the War Department directing a board to convene at Santa Fe on the 10th consisting of Major Whiting, Colonel Lane, and Colonel DuBois, all of the Third, to examine Alex for promotion. He has accepted his appointment of Major, Ninth Cavalry, and we leave the 6th for Santa Fe to attend to this business.[16]

December 8
Santa Fe

We left Union day before yesterday in an ambulance, where we made ourselves very comfortable by sitting down on the bottom on a pile of blankets and buffalo robes. Mrs. Whiting accompanied us. The first night we stopped at Tecolote, a little Mexican town. The next day we came forty miles further to Kosoloski's, a ranch about twenty-seven miles from Santa Fe.[17] They gave us a delightful supper and breakfast consisting of trout, broiled turkey, omelette, potatoes, etc. Old Kosoloski's ranch is about three-fourths of a mile from the old Pecos Church, which we intend to visit on our return.

We arrived at this ancient town this afternoon and took up our abode at the Fonda on the corner of the plaza. We have, however, agreed to go to Colonel Kinzie's, the paymaster's, tomorrow.

December 9

This morning I went to church, quite a rare occurrence in this country. Service was held in a room in the building known as the "palace"—being the residence of the governor.

The clergyman was an old Presbyterian who has only been here two or three weeks.

Some time ago, the Protestants of the place had succeeded in building quite a large church, but the day before the services were first held in it the roof fell in. The Catholics considered it a visitation from heaven, but the Protestants were inclined to attribute it to the perfidy of the Mexican builders under the influence of their priests. This misfortune seemed to have dampened the zeal of the few Protestants of the city, and the church remains in the same dilapidated condition.[18]

In the afternoon I went with Mrs. Kinzie to the cathedral, an old adobe edifice curious from its antiquity.

December 12

This being Saint Guadeloupe's [sic] day, in the evening the town was generally illuminated in honor of the saint, and bonfires were built at the corners of the streets. A large bonfire was also kindled on the flat roof of the church of Saint Guadeloupe in the lower part of the town which shed its light for some distance. The Mexicans have many saint days which, besides the church services, are celebrated by illuminations, fireworks, etc.

I took a walk all around the town yesterday with Dr. Huntington. He pointed out to me the most ancient parts of the city and especially part of the old pueblo, still standing, which was here when the Spaniards first founded the city of Santa Fe, the second oldest in the United States. The city is not as curious and interesting in appearance as Taos, as here the American element is decidedly visible.

December 13

Went this evening to a party at Governor Mitchell's, where I met all the American ladies and gentlemen of the city. A very pleasant affair. After twelve I started with Andrew and Colonel McClure for a Mexican baile which was taking place the same night. Unfortunately, however, we were too late for it.

Went with Mrs. Kinzie today to visit the convent. It

was exceedingly neat and well arranged, and the gardens in the interior are very fine. Found Sister Catharine, an old woman about fifty, in the depths of woe over the death of a canary bird. The heart will cling to some perishable thing when separated from the natural objects of its affection. With old Sister Catharine, her flowers and birds are in the stead of husband and children.

December 19

Left Santa Fe this morning and drove to Kosoloski's. Visited the ruins of Pecos. The old church is nearly all that remains. It is built in the form of a cross, the beams are of cedar, widely but elaborately carved. It must have been a finer church in its day than any now in Santa Fe. It is larger than the cathedral there. It was probably built by the Spaniards in the sixteenth century, but there is no tradition of this or of the inhabitants of Pecos. The estoffes near show that they combined the Aztec with the Christian worship, as the Pueblos still do. The church is of adobe, hard as rock, the walls immensely thick, the timber perfectly sound.

Time has not dealt with the old ruin as hardly as the hand of man; it is now being gradually demolished and the adobes and rafters put to baser uses. I brought away with me some of the carved wood and the head of a little Aztec image found among the ruins.[19]

December 25
Christmas Day, Ft. Union

We found orders awaiting us on our return from Santa Fe to take post at Fort Bascom, so this Christmas morning found us in the confusion incident to our moving tomorrow. In the morning went to church with Andrew. Mr. Morte has arranged a very nice little chapel here in the building of the Sons of Temperance. It was very prettily trimmed with greens and looked really like Christmas.

On our return from church I had all the noncommissioned officers of G Company to take eggnog and lunch with us. A sort of farewell to G Company. It passed off very successfully.

Our thoughts and conversations have been today of Willowbrook, where they are having such a merry gathering, and of Croquet Cottage, where we were all so happy a year ago. Keogh is captain, Seventh Cavalry, which is a great comfort and satisfaction to me.[20] My other boys are doing well also, I hear.

December 31
Fort Bascom
    We were four days and a half coming from Union and arrived here early yesterday morning. We camped out every night, always in wild and beautiful locations. A winter camp was quite a novelty to me and presented a beautiful picture with the numerous campfires lighting up the pines, or the huge cottonwoods, and the white tents gleaming in the moonlight. We had a Sibley tent and stove and were quite comfortable, though the weather was right cold for camping out.
    We found Captains Hawley and McMullen at this post, who received us very hospitably.

January 1, 1867
    The New Year finds us quite comfortably established at Fort Bascom, a neat little post in the southeastern part of New Mexico on the Canadian river. Being on the Comanche frontier, it is a post of some importance. The climate is mild and pleasant, and it is seldom visited by the windstorms which hold such sway at Union. The quarters are too small, but still warm and comfortable.[21]
    We took our New Year's dinner today with the surgeon, Dr. Weisse, and his wife. Had a very quiet day, not diversified by many *calls*.

January 7
    This morning Andrew started off on a scout with all the cavalry officers, expecting to be gone four days. The Navajo Indians have been running off from the reservation at Sumner and molesting and killing the cattle herders on the Red River, so this scout is in search of them.

January 10

Andrew returned this evening, bringing me three fine bows and a panther skin quiver full of arrows. He had had a very tiresome trip and captured seven Navajos. One, a squaw, he let go. The others begged so hard for mercy he had not the heart to follow out his instructions and kill them. So after marching them under guard a couple of days and terrifying them until they began to howl and sing their death songs, he let them escape the night before he got here. He did not wish to bring them to Bascom, as the illusion would then be destroyed, as they would probably be sent back to the Bosque in a couple of weeks. He wished them to believe it was certain death to be caught away from the reservation.[22]

January 14

This morning Andrew and I, accompanied by Captain Hawley, started for Sumner. We went as far as Hobbles' ranch —forty-five miles, a good ride, and rather more than our mules fancied.

A few miles from the ranch we came upon some very curious salt lakes, or ponds. At first sight they had the appearance of being completely frozen over, but on nearer approach they proved to be entirely covered with a thick crust of salt. I learn there are several other salt lakes in the vicinity, some yielding a very fine quality of salt. Fort Bascom gets its supply from one, the salt being cut out in thick cakes.

January 15

Today we traveled ten or fifteen miles on the Llano Estacado, crossing the extreme northwestern portion of it. We found both the ascent and descent from the tableland very steep and precipitous. When we had acsended the llano, we found ourselves on a flat plain extending south and east as far as the eye could see, covered with a short, tufty grass, and without sign of bush or tree. The soil was hard and firm as if long baked by the sun. This is the general character of the Staked Plain, excepting where it borders on the Canadian, where it assumes a heavy, sandy character. We saw no signs of game, excepting bands of antelope, which were hovering around in the distance. The want of water prevents it from being a resource for other game, but the antelope seems to care as little for water as a prairie dog.

We marched thirty-five miles and reached Fort Sumner or the "Bosque Redondo" at 2 P.M. I must say I never saw such an undesirable location for a post, and especially for a large Indian reservation. The country was almost as flat and as destitute of trees as the Staked Plain. The only trees to be seen were a few cottonwoods bordering the Pecos River, a round clump of which, near the fort, give the place the name of Bosque Redondo or "round woods."

When we approached within four miles of the fort, we found quite an improvement in the appearance of things. Wide acequias extended here and there, many large fields were under cultivation, and a wide and handsome avenue, six miles long bordered on each side with young trees, [which] made a very fine entrance to the post. As we drove in, our attention was attracted by the novel sight of Indians at work(!) hoeing in the corn fields.

The post presented a very military appearance, everything being neat and in fine order. It is garrisoned by four companies of the Fifth Infantry and two of the Third Cavalry and is commanded by General Sykes, lieutenant colonel of the Fifth. The quarters are of adobe and well arranged. The parade is of earth (hardened by frequent drilling), as grass will not grow in this locality, they tell me.

January 16

This morning early General Sykes called and invited me to go up and see their rations distributed to the Indians, as this was ration day, so about 10 A.M. we rode up in the ambulance to the ration house at the further end of the avenue. The day was the most delicious I have seen this winter (which has been charming weather continuously), warm and balmy as a morning in spring.

When we arrived, we found most of the Indians had left,

but there were several hundred waiting for their rations still —a motley crowd of bucks and squaws and papooses, all well wrapped up, some in government blankets, some in their own variegated, ingenious Navajo blankets. Most of them had a liberal allowance of bright beads adorning them. The men were of much taller stature than the Utes or the Pueblos, and some of the women were decidedly good looking, with large, soft black eyes. There are now eight thousand Navajos on this reservation. As most of them are prisoners of war, I expected to find them of a sullen and unhappy appearance, but on the contrary those I saw looked very contented and cheerful.

There is a popular illusion to the effect that Indians never laugh. I have seen several assertions of this kind in different books. Anyone who had been at the ration distribution today would have had their ideal of "Jo's" stolidity rudely shaken if they had seen the merriment excited throughout the crowd by the antics of one old Indian who came away laden with a tripe in addition to his ration. And I remember when I was at Garland and saw the presents distributed to the Utes, those wild children of the forest indulged in uproarious laughter when several barrels of brown sugar were emptied in the middle of the court and everyone was allowed to grab for it.

The rations to the Navajos are distributed every other day. Formerly they used to issue ten days' rations at once. There were then one thousand Apaches on the reservation; but one morning, having received their ten days' supply, they took french leave and have not appeared since. There are now only some ten Apaches on the reservation.[23] These are noted for the ingenious baskets they make of the Spanish bayonets, while the Navajos excel in their famous blankets. The daily ration they give is three-fourths of a pound of flour and meat and a handful of salt to each Indian, little and big. Not much to support life on, one would think.

The reservation around the post is forty miles square, but as I have before mentioned the only naturally growing trees are the few cottonwoods along the Pecos, which are forbidden to be cut. The consequence is that the Indians suffer from the want of fuel, their chief supply being the roots they dig with

great labor out of the ground. This is one of the great draw-
backs of the Bosque; another is the abominable water of the
Pecos river (the only supply the post has), which is very
brackish.[24]

January 17

Today I went out with Colonel DuBois and Lieutenant
and Mrs. Lee to visit one of the huts of the Navajos. In the
distance a plain covered with these huts has all the appearance
of a field in haying covered with little round hillocks of hay.
One could hardly believe they [were] gazing upon human habitations.

We saw one of the huts in process of construction. A circular place was dug about three feet deep and about ten in
diameter; around the edge of this boughs were stuck into the
ground and bending over tied together at the centre. Upon this,
dirt and mud is laid which hardens in the sun, and the simple
structure is completed. They build their small fire in the middle
of the floor, and the smoke escapes through an opening in the
roof.

I entered one of the huts, stooping as I passed through the
low doorway and reminded of the "snow houses" with their
low doors we used to build when we were children. One could
stand erect very comfortably in the centre of the hut. There
were seven or eight Indians there, some of them children. Some
of them had just come to the reservation in a party of four
hundred who delivered themselves up at Fort Wingate a few
weeks ago.[25] As they had yet no habitation, they had been hospitably invited by some of their old acquaintances to stay with
them. The "mistress of the mansion" was seated crosslegged
in the middle of the floor, busily engaged in weaving a small
blanket on a loom which was erect before her. We watched
her progress with a great deal of interest and wondered from
whence the Navajo derived their curious skill in weaving. Is it
a remnant of the Aztec civilization which once flourished in
the land? Some of the blankets they make are very fine and of
handsome design and sell for several hundred dollars. They
are made so firm and compact that one can carry water in them

any distance without the least moisture being visible on the outside.

The Navajos in their native country beyond the Rio Grande were a wealthy tribe. Besides cultivating the ground extensively, they owned large flocks and herds. Some of the Navajo sheep were very curious, having six horns. I believe some of these are still extant in the country.

VII

An Inspection Tour
and Ordered Home

Forts Bascom and Union, February–April, 1867

[*Editor's note:* Eveline's diary abruptly stops with the preceding entry. In order to round out the narrative of the Alexanders' tour of duty in New Mexico, the following entries have been abstracted from letters in the Booher Collection.]

February 16, 1867
Fort Bascom

Last evening's mail brought us ten or fifteen newspapers, a Littell, the Spanish Pilgrim's Progress, besides letters of January 21st and 22nd and others. The most important letter, though, was one Andrew received from Comstock. Andrew, in a previous letter, had suggested to him the propriety of sending out an honest inspector to this country, to look into the matter of beef contracts and one thing and another, in which there has been considerable fraud. To Andrew's surprise, and somewhat to his dismay, Comstock tells him that Grant has issued an order directing him to make such an inspection and afterwards report in person at Washington.[1] The order has not yet arrived, but I suppose will come by next mail. Until we see how extensive the inspection is to be, we cannot tell how long it will take, probably not beyond the last of April, if that long. This, of course, settles the question of our being ordered direct to Texas from here. It also has another advantage: Andrew will now be able to be my escort all the way home while before he expected to leave me at Saint Louis and go on at once to

New Orleans. I must say, though, that otherwise this inspection business is somewhat of a nuisance, for it will keep Andrew running around the country during the remainder of our stay in New Mexico, and the exposure of frauds is a business neither agreeable nor popular.

We are both perfectly well; indeed, I have not even an uncomfortable feeling to complain of. I received a week ago [the] Life of Havelock and Robertson's Sermons, which were both most acceptable. Andrew and I have both finished reading Havelock, and it is now doing duty in the company. Jim writes me he took a little talk out of it when it was in Saint Louis.

I think you had best direct our letters after this to Fort Union, as we may break up here in a week or two, and wherever we are they will be forwarded to us from Union.

You ask me about Livingstone and Willis. The former is recovering rapidly—the other slowly. Willis will not return to G Company, as his term of service is already expired. I don't know how it is with Livingstone. We hear of them occasionally through the doctor at Garland.[2]

We have heartily congratulated ourselves on our last move since we have become settled here, for the charming weather we have enjoyed is a great improvement on the wind of Union. We have had a snowstorm this week in which two or three inches fell and gave the post for a day or two quite the appearance of winter. It was a curious storm, accompanied by thunder and lightning, a phenomenon I never remember before in a snowstorm.

Andrew went hunting today and brought me in eleven blue quail. These are a different variety from the eastern quail and are very nice.

If I see Francisco again before I leave the country, I will ask him what he will take for the Fort Stevens plateau. I think, however, I would rather own one of the Spanish Peaks. I know the gentleman that owns them, Colonel St. Vrain, and I think he would let me have one cheap. When Andrew was hunting in the Smoky Mountains (East Tennessee), he met an old hunter, Jim Walker, who had bought ten thousand acres on top of the Smoky range. He had paid $1.50 (registry fee) for the claim, and enjoyed his aerial possessions wonderfully. I must say, though, I don't share your desire to make my home west of the Mississippi river. It is an interesting country to visit, but a hard one to settle in.

March 14, 1867
Fort Bascom

Much to my surprise, yesterday morning Andrew made his appearance. He found that it would take him until the last of April to get through with this inspection, as he has to go down to El Paso, and concluded to send me to Santa Fe to remain till he was ready to start in, as he could not make up his mind to leave me so long alone at this lonely post. We start tomorrow morning for Fort Sumner, where he will be detained several days; from there I will go with an escort to Santa Fe, and he will go to Fort Stanton and from there to Fort Bliss,[3] and from that point to Santa Fe, visiting all the posts up the river. I am going to stay with Major and Mrs. Whiting until Andrew returns from this tour, and as we will not go to housekeeping again, I have sent the greater part of our "plunder" direct to Fort Union to await our arrival there. So I have the comforting assurance that I am already well packed up for the states, which is a very comfortable feeling. I have arranged my packing so that all my housekeeping arrangements can be left at Saint Louis and stored there until we need them, and then if we are stationed somewhere down the river, they can be sent to us at little expense. Our horses and dogs we will leave in Saint Louis, excepting Maida, whom I think I shall bring home for Violet, if I can.

I am very much pleased to remain with the Whitings while Andrew is away, for they are both very pleasant and agreeable people. As soon as Andrew returns we will start in by the Raton Route, as Andrew has to inspect the post at Maxwell's. As we will have a good escort, there will probably be quite a number who will avail themselves of this opportunity to go in, and it will make quite a pleasant party.

March 29, 1867
Fort Union

I find this is quite a different climate from Bascom, as we are several hundred feet higher up in the world. There are several inches of snow on the ground—more than I have seen at any time this winter. March, though, is a disagreeable month everywhere. I have never yet been where it was not accompanied by unpleasant winds.[4]

I am very comfortable and contented here. I have a large, well-furnished room just off the parlour, with a cheerful open fire in it. I am now writing in the parlour. Captain Shoemaker is alike engaged at the same table. We are at the Arsenal, about a mile from the post, which is near enough whenever I want any society, but I am quite contented with the old gentleman and Sam (the latter is about twenty-two, I should think) and don't care to go visiting much. I am busily engaged in sewing and mending, as my clothes are beginning to give out a little.[5]

Captain Shoemaker has a buggy and pair of horses, with which he takes me to drive whenever the wind does not blow too hard. I have not heard from Andrew yet, and shall not for a week or more. I suppose he will be at El Paso by the last of this month. It will take him several days to go there from Fort Stanton.

We heard from Colonel Hatch, colonel of the Ninth, a few weeks ago. He says the Ninth is to start for the Texas frontier the first of April and said the regiment was finally armed and equipped. He did not say what part of Texas they were to be stationed in.[6]

I have all my things packed, which is quite a relief to my mind. I sold my stove and my crockery, as I thought the money was easier to pack around than the articles; at all events the transportation would cost less. When Andrew returned to Bascom, he told me he had given our stove to Mrs. Sutorious and was quite astonished and amused when I told him I had sold it! We gave twenty dollars for it at Little Rock, and after having used it a year and lost more than half the pots and kettles, I sold it for fifteen dollars, which I think was doing very well. You see, I am getting to be quite a manager. I am now trying to sell my ambulance![7]

April 21
Fort Union

I am looking for Andrew the last of this week—you can imagine with how much pleasure. He probably reached Santa Fe today. Everyone is astonished at the rapidity with which he has gone through with this inspection tour, and a good many sly jokes have been perpetrated as to the wonderful impetus it gives a man to leave his wife behind him. I expect Andrew has missed me more than I have him, for I have been amused and busy all the time, while he has been obliged to spend day after day poking along behind four mules in an ambulance.

I got a real "love letter" from him the other day, written in pencil in the ambulance while he was resting the mules, and I replied to it in some haste, as I was wishing to catch the mail. I was amused afterwards, as I thought of the way I had answered his letter of sentiment. Mine was full of instructions to "write to Mulford at Sumner, to send up Errickson and the horses, to get a furlough at Santa Fe for the soldier who is going in with us and various reminders of pay accounts, and a postscript to the effect not to forget to get a bushel of corn meal to feed the dogs going in." Well, you see he has to attend to Uncle Sam's interests, and it is as well for one of us to look after the family affairs.

The weather has been perfectly lovely the last few days, and everyone says we have every prospect of fine weather for crossing the plains. I must say I am longing to be living again in the open air. It oppresses me to stay in the house these delicious days, and I shall be glad enough to exchange my comfortable bedroom for a tent. I rather dreaded the journey as I thought of it some time ago, but now that the time approaches for us to start, I look forward to it with very pleasant anticipation. I am glad to go in by the Raton route, for I want to get a parting look at the Spanish Peaks and enjoy again the glorious scenery of the Raton mountains. After we leave them and are once more on the plains, our route will be somewhat monotonous, but the road from there is, they say, smooth as a barn-floor and that *under the circumstances* should console us for the absence of mountain scenery.[8]

I am as well and hearty as ever, and have been ever since Andrew left me. I expect him here the 25th or the 26th [and we shall then leave shortly for the states].

Ever fondly yours,
Evy

APPENDIX

Officers of the U.S. Army
Mentioned in the Journal

UNLESS otherwise noted, the information given below is abstracted from Francis B. Heitman, *Historical Register and Dictionary of the United States Army from Its Organization, September 29, 1789, to March 2, 1903*. The volume and page numbers at the end of each entry refer to the appropriate citation in that work.

AUDENRIED, JOSEPH CRAIN, of Pennsylvania. Graduate, U.S. Military Academy, 1861. Served with the First, Third, and Sixth cavalries. Breveted lieutenant colonel in 1865. In 1866 he became aide-de-camp to General W. T. Sherman and served in that capacity until his death in June, 1880. (I, 175.)

BANKHEAD, HENRY CLAY, of Maryland. Graduate, U.S. Military Academy, 1850. Served with various infantry companies until 1863, when he was named assistant inspector general. He served in that capacity until 1865. At the end of the Civil War, Bankhead transferred to the cavalry and served with that branch until his retirement in 1879. Breveted brigadier general for services during the Civil War, he was also cited for gallantry in action during various Indian campaigns. (I, 189.)

BARLOW, JOHN WHITNEY, of New York. Graduate, U.S. Military Academy, 1861. Served with the Topographical Engineers. At the time of the visit to Colorado he was captain and brevet lieutenant colonel of engineers. (Since one of Sherman's goals on the 1866 trip was an assessment of rail and wagon routes, this was undoubtedly one of the reasons Barlow was included in the party.) When Barlow retired in 1901, he held the rank of brigadier general and chief of engineers. (I, 191.)

BARNARD, ROBERT WILLIAM, of Washington, D.C. Joined the Nineteenth U.S. Infantry as first lieutenant in 1861 and served with that unit and as colonel of the 101st U.S. Colored Infantry until the end of the Civil War, when he was mustered out of the service. In September, 1865, he rejoined the army as captain of infantry and served until his death in July, 1870. At the time of the Alexanders' visit to Fort Smith, Barnard was the post commander. (I, 192; and Edwin C. Bearss and Arrell M. Gibson, *Fort Smith: Little Gibraltar on the Arkansas*, p. 309.)

CAIN, WILLIAM JESSE, of Vermont. Served as quartermaster sergeant of the Second Vermont until 1863, when he was commissioned a second lieutenant in the Third Infantry. Reassigned to the Third Cavalry in 1863, he served with that unit until he was mustered out of the service in 1870. (I, 273.)

CARLETON, JAMES HENRY, of Maine. One of the most famous figures in the history of the U.S. Army in the West, he served with the First Dragoons from 1839 to 1847 and then was assigned as colonel, First California Infantry. He became brigadier general of volunteers in April, 1862. Carleton served for many years in New Mexico and was always a controversial and stormy figure. Mustered out of service in 1866, he died in 1873. (I, 282. Most histories of the Indian campaigns in the West during the 1860's contain considerable information on Carleton.)

CARROLL, HENRY, of New York. Served as sergeant of artillery from 1859 to 1864, when he was commissioned a second lieutenant in the Third Cavalry. Served with various cavalry units from that time until his retirement in 1899, at which time he had been promoted to brigadier general of volunteers and cited several times for gallant service against the Indians in Texas and New Mexico. (I, 286.)

CASEY, JAMES S., of Pennsylvania. Served as private, New York State Militia, during 1861 until he was commissioned second lieutenant, Fifth Infantry. He was awarded the Medal of Honor for service against the Indians at Wolf Mountain, Montana, in 1877 and retired in 1897 with the rank of colonel. (I, 289.)

CHURCHILL, JAMES O., of Massachusetts. Joined the service as sergeant, Illinois Infantry, in 1861. Commissioned a second lieutenant in September, 1861, he served with various infantry companies until 1864, when he was appointed captain and assistant quartermaster of volunteers. He was serving as quartermaster at Fort Smith during the Alexanders' visit in 1866. (I, 301.)

COMSTOCK, CYRUS BALLOU, of Massachusetts. Graduate, U.S. Military Academy, 1865. Served with the Corps of Engineers until 1863, when he was named assistant inspector general. In 1864 Comstock became aide-de-camp to General Grant, and he served in that post from 1864 to 1870. He then returned to the Corps of Engineers and served until his retirement in 1895. (I, 319.)

CRESSY, EDWARD POTTER, of New York. Graduate, U.S. Military Academy, 1858. Served with the Mounted Rifles and the Third Cavalry. Honorably mustered out of service in January, 1871. (I, 338.)

DAVIDSON, JOHN WYNN, of Virginia. Graduate, U.S. Military Academy, 1845. Served with the First Dragoons until 1861, when he was assigned to the First Cavalry. Named brigadier general of volunteers in 1862, he served in that capacity until 1866, when he became lieutenant colonel, Tenth Cavalry, and served with various cavalry units until his death in 1881. (I, 355.)

DAYTON, LEWIS MULFORD, of New York. Joined the service as captain of volunteers in March, 1863, and served as assistant adjutant general until 1865. From August, 1866, to March, 1869, he was lieutenant colonel and military secretary to General W. T. Sherman. Discharged in 1870, at his own request, he died in 1891. (I, 362.)

DuBOIS, JOHN VAN DEUSEN, of New York. Graduate, U.S. Military Academy, 1855. Served with the Mounted Rifles until 1861, when that unit was redesignated the Third Cavalry. Thereafter he served as an artillery and cavalry officer until his retirement in May, 1876. (I, 385.)

DUTTON, EVERALL FLETCHER, of Massachusetts. First lieutenant, Illinois Infantry, 1861. Served with various Illinois units until the end of the Civil War. Breveted brigadier general for gallant and meritorious service in several campaigns. (I, 391. There are several Duttons who served during this period. This is probably the one Evy refers to in the diary.)

ENOS, HERBERT MERTON, of New York. Graduate, U.S. Military Academy, 1852. Served with the Mounted Rifles and several cavalry units until he was appointed to the Quartermaster Corps in 1861. Much of his service was spent in New Mexico, and many of the 1860 maps of the territory were prepared under his direction. Enos retired in 1876. (I, 407.)

FLOYD-JONES, DE LANCY, of New York. Graduate, U.S. Military Academy, 1841. Served with various infantry units until his retirement in 1879. Floyd-Jones was cited for gallantry at the battle of Molino del Rey, Mexico, and was breveted for gallantry and meritorious service at Gettysburg. (I, 426.)

FORSYTH, GEORGE ALEXANDER, of Pennsylvania. Enlisted as a private in 1861 and promoted to first lieutenant, Illinois Cavalry. Served with various volunteer cavalry companies until mustered out of service in 1866. He rejoined the army as major, Ninth Cavalry, in July, 1866. From 1869 to 1881 he served in various capacities on General Philip Sheridan's staff. Breveted brigadier general for gallantry and meritorious service in an engagement with hostile Indians on the Republican River, 1868. (I, 430.)

GARRARD, KENNER, of Kentucky. Graduate, U.S. Military Academy, 1847. Served with artillery and dragoon units until the beginning of the Civil War. During the war he served with various cavalry units and as colonel, 146th New York Infantry. Breveted major general of volunteers for conspicuous gallantry, he resigned in November, 1866. (I, 447–448.)

HARWOOD, PAUL, of Pennsylvania. Enlisted as a private in the New York militia and was later appointed second lieutenant of artillery. Mustered out in 1864, he rejoined the army as major, Fifty-seventh U.S. Colored Infantry, and served with that unit for some months before transferring to the Twenty-seventh Infantry. Retired in 1891. (I, 508–509.)

HATCH, EDWARD, of Maine. Served during the Civil War with the Second Iowa Cavalry, rising rapidly from the rank of captain to brigadier general of volunteers. Mustered out in 1866, he rejoined the army as colonel, Ninth Cavalry. (I, 510. See also William H. Leckie, *The Buffalo Soldiers: A Narrative of the Negro Cavalry in the West*, for a summary of Hatch's distinguished service with the Ninth.)

HAWLEY, WILLIAM, of Washington, D.C. Joined the army as a private in the Washington, D.C., Volunteer Infantry. In 1861 he was promoted to second lieutenant, Third Cavalry, and served with the Third until 1879, when he was named major, Fourth Cavalry. (I, 513.)

HOWE, MARSHALL SAXE, of Maine. Attended the U.S. Military Academy from 1823 to 1827 and then served with the First Dragoons until 1861, when he was named colonel, Third Cavalry. He retired shortly after the Third arrived in New Mexico. (I, 547–548. See also Ralph C. Deibert, *A History of the Third United States Cavalry*, p. 64.)

HOWLAND, GEORGE WASHINGTON, of Rhode Island. Graduate, U.S. Military Academy, 1848. Served with the Mounted Rifles and the Third Cavalry until his retirement in 1869. He served in New Mexico during the Civil War and was breveted for gallantry during the battle of Valverde, New Mexico. (I, 549.)

HUNTINGTON, DAVID LOWE, of Massachusetts. Served as assistant surgeon and major during the Civil War. Continued to hold various posts with the Surgeon General's Department until his retirement in 1898. (I, 558. See also Lydia Spencer Lane, *I Married A Soldier: Or Old Days in the Army*, p. 141.)

INMAN, HENRY, of New York. Enlisted as a private, Ninth Infantry, 1837. Promoted to lieutenant, Seventeenth Infantry, 1861, and later served as regimental quartermaster. Breveted lieutenant colonel for meritorious service against the Indians in 1869, he was cashiered in 1872. (I, 563.)

KEMBLE, JAMES R., of Pennsylvania. Joined the army as second lieutenant, Third Cavalry, and served with that unit until his death in 1869. (I, 591.)

KEOGH, MYLES W., of Ireland. Captain and aide-de-camp, April, 1862, and served in similar capacities until honorably mustered out in September, 1866. Breveted lieutenant colonel, he rejoined the army in 1866 as second lieutenant, Fourth Cavalry. Transferred to the Seventh Cavalry in July, 1866, and served with that unit until his death in June, 1876, at the battle of the Little Big Horn. (I, 593.)

KINZIE, ROBERT ALLEN, of Illinois. Joined the army as major and paymaster in 1861. Breveted lieutenant colonel in 1865 for faithful and meritorious service. Died in 1873. (I, 603.)

LANE, WILLIAM BARTLETT, of Kentucky. Served in the ranks of the Mounted Rifles from 1846 to 1848. Breveted lieutenant in 1848 and served throughout the Civil War with the Third Cavalry. Retired in 1870 with the rank of brevet colonel. (I, 614. See also the reminiscences of his wife, Lydia S. Lane, *I Married a Soldier*.)

LEE, CHARLES CARROLL, of Pennsylvania. Assistant surgeon, First Maryland Cavalry, 1861. Assistant surgeon, U.S. Army, 1862, until his retirement in 1867. (I, 623.)

LEE, JOHN DEMPSTER, of New York. Sergeant, New York Mounted Rifles, 1861. Later served as lieutenant of cavalry. Mustered out in 1865, he rejoined the army in 1866 as second lieutenant, Third Cavalry, and served in that unit until his death in 1867. (I, 625.)

LOCKWOOD, HENRY CLAY, of New York. Captain and aide-de-camp, 1862. Breveted major of volunteers in 1865 for gallantry at the storming of Fort Fisher, North Carolina. Honorably mustered out in 1866. (I, 638. Again, it is difficult to know for certain which of several Lockwoods Evy is referring to, but this is probably her "Major Lockwood.")

MARSHALL, ELISHA GAYLORD, of New York. Graduate, U.S. Military Academy, 1845. Served with various infantry units until the Civil War, when he was named colonel of volunteers. Mustered out in 1865, he rejoined the army as major, Fifth Infantry, and retired in 1867 with the rank of colonel. (I, 690.)

McGINNIS, JOHN RANDOLPH, of Ireland. Graduate U.S. Military Academy, 1859. Served as lieutenant and captain of ordnance during the Civil War. Breveted for gallantry during operations before Charleston, South Carolina, he retired in 1902 with the rank of colonel. (I, 666.)

MCMULLIN, GEORGE ORD (Eveline incorrectly spells his name MCMULLEN), of Pennsylvania. Joined the army as second lieutenant, Eighth Pennsylvania Cavalry, and served with various units during the Civil War. Second lieutenant, Third Cavalry, 1863. Honorably mustered out in 1871. (I, 678.)

MERRITT, WESLEY, of New York. Graduate, U.S. Military Academy, 1855. Served with the Second Dragoons and various cavalry units until 1863, when he was named brigadier general of volunteers. Honorably mustered out in 1866, he rejoined the army as lieutenant colonel, Ninth Cavalry, in 1866 and later served with the Fifth Cavalry. He was major general at the time of his retirement in 1900. (I, 706. See also Leckie, *Buffalo Soldiers*.)

MOALE, EDWARD, of Maryland. Joined the army as first lieutenant, Nineteenth Infantry, in 1861 and served as regimental quartermaster and later as lieutenant colonel and assistant adjutant general. In 1866 he transferred to the Thirty-seventh Infantry and served with various infantry units until his retirement in 1902. (I, 718.)

MULFORD, LAMBERT L., of New Jersey. Served with the Second New Jersey Cavalry from 1863 to 1864. Mustered out in 1865, he was appointed second lieutenant, Third Cavalry, and served with that unit until he was honorably mustered out in January, 1871. (I, 734.)

QUINTANA, NICHOLAS. Major, First New Mexico Volunteer Infantry. Quintana never served with the regular armed forces, and therefore Heitman provides no biographical sketch. (II, 139.)

RAWLES, JACOB BEEKMAN, of Michigan. Graduate, U.S. Military Academy, 1856. Served with various artillery units during and after the Civil War. Breveted major for gallant and meritorious service, he was promoted to brigadier general at the time of his retirement in 1903. (I, 817.)

RUSSELL, GERALD, of Ireland. Joined the army in 1851 as a private in the Mounted Rifles. In 1862 he was named acting second lieutenant, Third Cavalry, and served with that unit until 1867, when he was named major, Fifth Cavalry. Retired 1890. (I, 853.)

SHOEMAKER, WILLIAM RAWLE, of Pennsylvania. Joined the army in 1841 as an ordnance storekeeper and served in that capacity until his retirement in 1882. (I, 884. See also note 5, chapter 7.)

STANWOOD, FRANK, of Maine. Second lieutenant, Third Cavalry, from 1861 until his death in 1872. (I, 916.)

STEWART, JAMES H., of New York. Served with the California Volunteer Infantry during the Civil War and as lieutenant and captain, Fifteenth Infantry, from 1866 to 1867. (I, 924. This again is one of the places where Evy is rather vague about name and rank. This particular Stewart best fits the description and circumstances of the diary.)

STONEMAN, GEORGE, of New York. Graduate, U.S. Military Academy, 1842. Pursued a distinguished career with the First Dragoons and Second Cavalry. In 1862 he became major general of volunteers and later chief of the Cavalry Bureau. Mustered out of volunteer service in 1866, he rejoined the army as colonel, Twenty-first Infantry, and served in various capacities with the army until 1883, when he resigned to enter politics. From 1883 to 1887 he was governor of California. He later served as Pacific Railroad commissioner. His army rank was reinstated by special act of Congress, and he retired in 1891. (I, 930. See also *Dictionary of American Biography*, IX, 92.)

SUTORIUS, ALEXANDER, of Switzerland. Joined the army in 1854 as chief bugler and later was named sergeant major of Mounted Rifles. Appointed second lieutenant, Third Cavalry, in 1863 and served with that unit in various capacities until his dismissal in 1876. (I, 69, 937.)

SYKES, GEORGE, of Maryland. Graduate, U.S. Military Academy, 1838. Served with various infantry units until 1861, when he was named brigadier general of volunteers. Mustered out of volunteer service in 1866, he was named colonel, Twentieth Infantry, and served with various infantry units until his death in 1880. (I, 941–942.)

TARLETON, ELISHA WARFIELD, of Kentucky. Joined the army as second lieutenant, Third Cavalry, and served with that unit until he was honorably discharged in 1870. (I, 944–945.)

THOMAS, PHILIP KEARNEY, of Michigan. Joined the army in 1861 as second lieutenant, Third Cavalry, and thereafter followed a rather checkered career. He was cashiered in April, 1866, reinstated in June, 1866, and again cashiered in December, 1867. Unfortunately, Heitman provides no further details. (I, 954.)

TILFORD, JOSEPH GREEN, of Kentucky. Graduate, U.S. Military Academy, 1847. Served with the Mounted Rifles and Third Cavalry until 1867, when he was appointed major, Seventh Cavalry. Breveted for gallantry at the battle of Valverde, New Mexico, Tilford retired in 1891. (I, 961.)

VAN VLIET, FREDERICK, of New York. Joined as second lieutenant, Third Cavalry, in 1861 and served with that unit throughout the Civil War. Named major, Tenth Cavalry, in 1882. Breveted lieutenant colonel in 1865 for gallant and meritorious service. (I, 984.)

VROOM, PETER DUMONT, of New Jersey. Served with various New Jersey infantry units during the Civil War. Honorably mustered out in 1865, he was appointed second lieutenant, Third Cavalry, in 1866 and served with the Third until he joined the inspector general's office in 1888. Retired in 1903 as brigadier general. (I, 990.)

WADE, JAMES FRANKLIN, of Ohio. Joined the Third Cavalry in 1861 and served with various cavalry units during the Civil War. After the war, Wade served with both the Ninth and the Tenth Cavalry. Promoted to major general in 1903 shortly before his retirement. (I, 991.)

WHITING, CHARLES JARVIS, of Massachusetts. Graduate, U.S. Military Academy, 1835. Served with various artillery and cavalry units through 1863. Appointed major, Third Cavalry, in 1866 and lieutenant colonel, Sixth Cavalry, in 1869. Honorably mustered out of service in 1871. (I, 1029. See also Lane, *I Married A Soldier*. Mrs. Lane frequently mentions Whiting and his wife, who were evidently very popular with the officers and their wives at Santa Fe.)

Notes

INTRODUCTION

1. Some of these memoirs have been published in several editions, and most are well known to western history enthusiasts. Among the most easily obtainable are William Tecumseh Sherman, *Memoirs of General William T. Sherman*; Philip H. Sheridan, *Personal Memoirs of P. H. Sheridan*; George Crook, *General George Crook: His Autobiography*; Captain R. G. Carter, *On the Border with Mackenzie; Or, Winning West Texas from the Comanches*; Thomas W. Sweeny, *Journal of Lt. Thomas W. Sweeny, 1849–1853*; Percival G. Lowe, *Five Years a Dragoon ('49 to '54) and Other Adventures on the Great Plains*; and Captain John G. Bourke, *On the Border with Crook*.

2. Robert M. Utley, "Arizona Vanquished," *The American West* 6 (November, 1969): 16.

3. Elizabeth B. Custer, *"Boots and Saddles"; Or, Life in Dakota with General Custer*, p. xxix.

4. There is a discrepancy in the spelling of Mrs. Alexander's Christian name. All of the family sources (including the Martin family Bible) indicate that she was named for her aunt, Evelina Martin Rochester, and give the spelling as Evelina. However, the Bancroft copy of the diary and various official documents (including Mrs. Alexander's pension application and will) give her name as Eveline. I have used Eveline for the convenience of scholars and researchers who will find her so listed in most printed sources and in the Bancroft catalog. Undoubtedly, however, her name was Evelina, although she may have changed the spelling later to conform with some clerical error. Within the family she was usually called Evy.

5. Again, as with the officers' memoirs listed above, there are several editions of most of these works. James Day, in his introduction to Teresa Vielé's book, gives a brief publication history of each, along with a comparative essay on the several authors. The best known include Elizabeth Custer, *"Boots and Saddles"*, *Following the Guidon*, and *Tenting on the Plains; Or, General Custer in Kansas and Texas*; Lydia Spencer Lane, *I Married a Soldier; Or, Old Days in the Army*; Teresa Vielé, *"Following the Drum": A Glimpse of Frontier Life*; Ellen McGowen Biddle, *Reminiscences of a Soldier's Wife*; and Martha Summerhayes,

Vanished Arizona: Recollections of the Army Life of a New England Woman.

6. Edward S. Martin, *Some Account of Family Stocks Involved in Life at Willowbrook*, p. 57. Most of the information on the Martin family comes from this valuable little volume of family reminiscenes.

7. In addition to his work with the *Lampoon*, Martin was the first editor of *Life* magazine, a well-known New York journalist, and an associate editor of *Harper's*. See *Who Was Who in America, 1897–1942*, p. 782.

8. James B. Wilson, *The Life and Services of Brevet Brigadier General Andrew Jonathan Alexander*, pp. 5–6.

9. Ibid., p. 92.

10. Letter, Eveline Alexander to her father, January 18, 1868, from the private collection of Mr. and Mrs. Edward E. Booher, Cranbury, N.J., and quoted with their kind permission.

11. Eveline Alexander to her mother, June 28, 1866, Booher Collection.

12. Eveline Alexander to her mother, December 16, 1866, Booher Collection.

13. For a description of Evy's life at Fort McDowell and excerpts from her Arizona letters, see Sandra L. Myres, "Evy Alexander: The Colonel's Lady at McDowell in Arizona," *Montana: The Magazine of Western History* 24 (Summer, 1974): 26–38.

14. Wilson, *Life and Services*; "Statement of the military service of Andrew J. Alexander," June 10, 1885, and "Proceedings of the Retiring Board Convened at Governor's Island, New York," June 19, 1885, filed with Pension Application File #335–245, 3632 ACP 1887, Record Group 94, National Archives, Washington, D.C.

15. Interviews and letters, Mrs. Eric (Sylvia) Maude, Mrs. Edward E. (Agnes) Booher, Miss Violet Wilder, and Mr. George Martin to the editor, January, 1972–June, 1974.

16. A brief biography of Upton, Evy's brother-in-law, and a summary of his career are in *Dictionary of American Biography*, X, 128–130. See also Stephen E. Ambrose, *Upton and the Army*.

17. Jane R. Stewart in Custer, *Following the Guidon*, p. xiii.

CHAPTER I

1. Willowbrook was the Martin family home near Auburn, New York. Built by Eveline's uncle, Governor Enos T. Throop, the property was purchased by Eveline's father, E. T. T. Martin, about 1840. Two delightful reminiscences of family life at Willowbrook are those written by Eveline's mother, Cornelia Williams Martin, *The Old Home*, and by her brother, Edward Sanford Martin, *Some Account of Family Stocks Involved in Life at Willowbrook*. The latter volume contains a sequel by G. W. Martin entitled "The Great Matriarchs," which includes details of Eveline Alexander's life at Willowbrook after her husband's death.

2. George and Ned (Edward) were Eveline's brothers. The other boys mentioned were from neighboring families along the Auburn–Owasco Road. Martin, *Life at Willowbrook*, p. 98.

Although the Martins attended the Sand Beach Dutch Reformed Church, where Eveline taught Sunday School, the family was more ecumenical than denominational. Edward recalled, "Mother was full of religion, colored by her church associations but not really sectarian, and she was coming out from dawn to dark, to save the world" (Martin, *Life at Willowbrook*, p. 59).

During Eveline's western "service," she and her mother were active in organizing missions and relief efforts for several Indian tribes and in attempting to find pastors for Protestant churches in western towns. See Sandra L. Myres, "Evy Alexander: The Colonel's Lady at McDowell in Arizona," *Montana: The Magazine of Western History* 24 (Summer, 1974).

3. General Cyrus Ballou Comstock, aide-de-camp to General U. S. Grant, was evidently a close family friend. Eveline's list of "Letters Sent and Received" frequently includes his name. Comstock and all other military officers mentioned in the diary are more fully identified in the appendix.

4. Eveline's description of her mother as "delicate" is at variance with Edward's remembrance. He describes Mrs. Martin as a lively, active woman with "purposes maturing in her mind every minute connected with all sorts of people and missions." She remained healthy and active until her death in 1899 at the age of eighty-one, so Eveline's fears for her mother's health were no doubt more influenced by the approaching separation than by any real illness. For a fuller description of Mrs. Martin, see Martin, *Life at Willowbrook*, pp. 60–64.

5. Again, Eveline seems overly concerned. As noted in the introduction, Eveline's uncle was Enos T. Throop, governor of New York from 1829 to 1832. Governor Throop died in November, 1874, at the age of ninety. For a fuller description of his career, see *Dictionary of American Biography*, IX, 510–511, and an article by Mrs. Martin, "Sketch of the Life of Governor Throop," *Cayuga County Historical Society Collection* 7 (1889): 155–167.

6. The reference here is to Alexander's sister Apolline and her husband, Francis P. Blair, Jr., a Missouri legislator and congressman and son of Jackson's famous "Kitchen Cabinet" member. As noted in the introduction the Martin and Blair families were close friends. For a sketch of Frank Blair, Jr., see *Dictionary of American Biography*, I, 332–334. The close ties between the two families are detailed in Martin, *The Old Home*, I, 41–45.

7. Eveline was accurate in her opinion of Odin. During the 1860's the town, located between Saint Louis and Vincennes, was known as the "hell-hole of the Illinois Central." Federal Writers' Project, *Illinois: A Descriptive and Historical Guide*, p. 617.

8. Thomas B. Lincoln of Hunt County, Texas, was a member of Captain W. R. Lane's Company, Fourteenth Brigade, Texas Militia. Confederate Pension Rolls, Texas State Archives.

9. Alexander served on General George Stoneman's staff during the Peninsular campaign, and when Stoneman was named to command the Cavalry Bureau in Washingotn, he selected Alexander as his adjutant-

general. During 1865 Alexander again served with Stoneman, this time as chief-of-staff. Another member of the staff was Myles Keogh.

The Stonemans took a personal interest in the young Alexanders; Eveline and Andrew were frequent guests at the Stoneman's home, and the two families maintained close contacts following the Civil War. The relationship between Stoneman and Alexander is traced in James B. Wilson, *The Life and Services of Brevet Brigadier General Andrew Jonathan Alexander*, pp. 17, 28–29.

10. During the 1860's De Vall's Bluff, about forty-five miles east of Little Rock on the western bank of the White River, was an active settlement and steamboat port. Federal Writers' Project, *Arkansas: A Guide to the State*, p. 226.

11. The standard army ambulance was a stout spring wagon equipped with leather-covered seats and covered with a canvas top supported on bows. Most cavalry regiments had two or three of these vehicles available not only to carry the sick and wounded but as passenger wagons for officers and their families. Both two- and four-wheeled models were available, and although Mrs. Alexander does not mention which hers was, the two-wheeled models were considered the most comfortable and were the most popular among the officers as carriages, pleasure vehicles, and transportation. A brief, illustrated description of the ambulance can be found in Sidney E. Whitman, *The Troopers: An Informal History of the Plains Cavalry, 1865–1890*, pp. 219–220.

12. Jack, christened John Williams, was another of Eveline's brothers. He was sixteen at the time the diary was written and was considered the family sportsman and hunter. Martin, *Life at Willowbrook*, p. 88.

13. The Fifty-seventh Regiment of Colored Infantry was one of the many Negro units formed late in the Civil War. Officered by whites, these troops were used primarily for garrison and guard duty and saw little active combat. The Fifty-seventh was organized in March, 1864, and assigned to the District of Eastern Arkansas.

Many Negro units were being mustered out of service in 1866, and the regiment's members may well have thought the New Mexico expedition would delay their release from federal service. As it turned out, the regiment made the long trip to New Mexico only to be ordered back to Arkansas and mustered out in December, 1866. For a brief history of the Fifty-seventh Regiment, see Frederick H. Dyer, *A Compendium of the War of the Rebellion*, III, 1733. A mention of the regiment's New Mexico service appeared in *The Santa Fe Weekly Gazette*, November 29, 1866.

14. The mutiny of the Fifty-seventh Regiment was widely reported in the Arkansas papers, and Colonel Marshall S. Howe filed a long report on it shortly after his arrival in New Mexico. Howe's account does not differ significantly from Eveline's, although it provides more details on the quelling of the mutiny. The mutineers were sent to Little Rock for trial but, as Eveline notes, were later returned to the expedition despite Howe's attempts to have them retained in Arkansas. Howe's report is in M. S. Howe to Captain Charles E. Howe, May 25, 1866, Letters Received by the District of New Mexico, H-71-1866, Record Group 393, National

Archives, Washington, D.C. There are also reports of the mutiny in Edwin C. Bearss and Arrell M. Gibson, *Fort Smith: Little Gibraltar on the Arkansas*, p. 309; and in George H. Shirk, ed., "The Lost Colonel," *Chronicles of Oklahoma* 35 (Summer, 1957): 180–181.

15. Molly was Eveline's oldest sister, Mary William Throop.

16. The reference here is to the famous cavalry officer Myles W. Keogh, who later served with the Seventh Cavalry and whose army career is briefly traced in the appendix. He and Alexander served together on Stoneman's staff, and the two became close friends. Keogh was a frequent visitor at Willowbrook, where he was quite popular with Eveline's sisters. Edward recalled, "I see him now sitting in the library by the glass door reading Charles O'Malley to a circle of girls sitting around and working at something" (Martin, *Life at Willowbrook*, pp. 83–84).

There is a persistent legend that Keogh was engaged to Eveline's sister Cornelia (Nelly). According to one historian of the Seventh Cavalry, Edward S. Luce: "This friendship caused Keogh to lose his heart. . . . Whether or not this deep friendship was prevented from culminating into anything deeper, we do not know. We do know Keogh never married. Neither did this young lady; and for 50 years after this Garry Owen entered his Valhalla, she remained true to his memory, later to be buried beside him" (Edward S. Luce, *Keogh, Comanche and Custer*, 23). Present members of the family discount the engagement as romantic myth rather than fact. However, following Keogh's death in the Battle of the Little Big Horn, the Alexanders had his body removed to Willowbrook and reinterred in the family plot at Auburn, New York. Luce's book contains a description of the reinterment service, taken from the *Auburn Morning News*, October 26, 1877.

CHAPTER II

1. Scullyville (or Skullyville) was a small settlement about ten miles southwest of Fort Smith. Established in 1832, the town served as the "educational, social, and political center of the Choctaw nation" and was the site of the New Hope School for girls. Devastated by Union troops during the Civil War, the settlement never regained its earlier prominence. Federal Writers' Project, *Oklahoma: A Guide to the Sooner State*, pp. 383–384.

2. This strange collection of canines was not unusual. Officers and men in the post–Civil War army kept an assorted collection of pets of all kinds, and almost any western army post during the late nineteenth century had a large population of dogs. Although hounds and hunting dogs were the most popular, fighting dogs, lap dogs, companion dogs, and just plain "dawgs" were also much in evidence. Sprightly accounts of army pets are found in W. S. Nye, *Carbine and Lance: The Story of Old Fort Sill*, pp. 285, 291; and Elizabeth B. Custer, *Following the Guidon*, pp. 112–130.

3. Eveline's "Indian lore" is a strange mixture of myth, half-truths, and fact. Like many Anglos, particularly those from the East, she tended to view all Indians as savages. However, the so-called Five Civilized Tribes, including the Choctaws, were sedentary, agricultural people with

highly developed native cultures. By the 1830 Treaty of Dancing Rabbit Creek, the Choctaws exchanged their lands east of the Mississippi River for all of the country that is now southern Oklahoma, and most of them had moved to their new homes by 1833. The Choctaws and the other related tribes lived in rural communities and operated small farms and ranches. They had their own governments, constitutions, and laws and were particularly noted for their excellent educational systems and schools.

The route followed by the Third Cavalry during the march to New Mexico passed through the Choctaw and Chickasaw nations and the so-called Leased District, an area west of the ninety-eighth meridian which was part of the Choctaw Nation but leased to the U.S. government in 1855 for the settlement of several tribes, including the Caddos and Hasinais. For a good summary of the history and peoples of those lands, see Muriel H. Wright, *A Guide to the Indian Tribes of Oklahoma.*

4. This was probably a book by the Reverend Archibald Bonar entitled *Sermons, Chiefly on Devotional Subjects,* published in Edinburgh, Scotland, in 1817.

5. Eveline's elaborate description of her "costume" for the journey is in interesting contrast to the statement of her "sister-in-arms," Lydia Spencer Lane, who also made a long trip to New Mexico in 1866. "It was amusing to an old campaigner like myself to see the brides start off from Fort Leavenworth for an ambulance expedition of six hundred miles," Mrs. Lane recalled. "Their dainty costumes were far more suitable for Fifth Avenue than camp and a hot, dusty ride in the broiling sun day after day. . . . I started out as I intended to dress throughout the march, —a calico frock, plainly made, no hoops, and a sun-bonnet. . . . [and] there was not a husband who did not commend my common-sense dress, urging their wives to adopt it" (Lane, *I Married a Soldier,* pp. 131–132).

6. Eveline remarks on some of the same characteristics of the southeastern Oklahoma landscape that attracted other observers. For example, Lieutenant A. W. Whipple, who visited the same section of the country in 1853–1854, commented: "The road traversed a country of well-wooded hills, with gentle slopes, and fine grassy prairies intervening. . . . The hills and plains abound in excellent timber, principally of oak. Small streams, or pools of water, are found in numerous ravines, and the meadows are covered with grass" (Grant Foreman, ed., *A Pathfinder in the Southwest: The Itinerary of Lieutenant A. W. Whipple,* pp. 38–39).

7. Under the terms of their treaties with the United States, the Choctaws (as well as the other civilized tribes) had their own governments, which had been heavily influenced by their long contact with Anglos. By 1866 the Choctaw Nation operated under a written constitution which provided for a system of inferior and superior courts and guaranteed trial by jury. According to contemporary observers, "Choctaw court procedure was smooth and regular, and the laws were well enforced" (Angie Debo, *The Rise and Fall of the Choctaw Republic,* p. 76). The scene witnessed by Lieutenant Mulford was probably a session of one of the county courts added to the Choctaw judicial system in 1850 for the trial of minor cases.

8. Beale's road was a route established in 1858 by Edward Fitzgerald Beale as part of the government's "Pacific wagon road" program. Beale's road followed earlier routes laid out by March and Simpson (1849-1850) and Whipple (1853). An account of the wagon road program and Beale's role in it is in W. Turrentine Jackson, *Wagon Roads West: A Study of Federal Road Surveys and Construction in the Trans-Mississippi West, 1846–1869*, pp. 241–256; and Stephen Bonsal, *Edward Fitzgerald Beale: A Pioneer in the Path of Empire, 1822–1903*.

9. This reference is to Eveline's older sister, Cornelia. Unfortunately Evy says nothing further about General Stoneman's white mule, so we can but wonder what adventures had befallen Nelly.

10. Emily is another sister who later joined Evy "in the army" as the wife of General Emory Upton.

11. The Whipple route was laid out by Lieutenant Amiel W. Whipple of the Topographical Engineers in 1853 as part of a series of surveys for a proposed railroad to the Pacific. Since the Alexanders generally followed Whipple's route, readers may be interested in comparing Evy's account and descriptions of the country with the observations made by Whipple and published in U.S. Congress, Senate, *Pacific Survey Reports*, III, 33d Cong., 2d sess., Exec. Doc. No. 78, or the newer edition of Whipple's itinerary edited and annotated by Foreman in *Pathfinder in the Southwest*. Another excellent description of the country traversed by the Alexanders is that by Whipple's topographer and artist H. Baulduin Möllhausen, *Diary of a Journey from the Mississippi to the Coasts of the Pacific with a United States Government Expedition*.

Fort Arbuckle, on the Washita River near present Davis, Oklahoma, was established in 1851. Captured by the Confederates in 1861, the fort was not reoccupied until late 1866. At this point in the journey, the Third Cavalry was about halfway between Fort Arbuckle on the Washita and old Camp Arbuckle on the Canadian River. See William Brown Morrison, "Fort Arbuckle," *Chronicles of Oklahoma* 6 (March, 1928): 26–34.

12. According to Thomas A. Muzzall, a hospital steward attached to the Fifty-seventh Infantry who was traveling with the first column, the march was about thirty-five miles. George Shirk, who edited and annoted Muzzall's brief account of the trip, places the two columns in the vicinity of Blanchard, Oklahoma, on July 4. George H. Shirk, ed., "The Lost Colonel," *Chronicles of Oklahoma* 35 (Summer, 1957): 185.

13. Howe obviously was not popular with the regimental officers. He had been kind to Eveline, and she found him "most amicable tho eccentric," but she commented that Howe had a reputation for being "more gallant in word than in deed." In a letter to her mother, Evy noted, "Colonel Howe with an indecision which is peculiarly trying to all, but which he manifests in everything, cannot make up his mind where he shall put the Negroes. . . . The difficulty with him is that he never commanded more than four companies before, he told me he never saw the whole regiment together until the review the other day, and now that he has two regiments to care for, it is too much for him" (Eveline Alexander to her mother, May 18, 1866, Booher Collection). Muzzall also comments on Howe's indecision and lack of popularity.

14. In several places in the journal Evy mentions Croquet Cottage and the Croquet family. She is probably referring to quarters which she and Andrew shared with several young officers, including Myles Keogh, in Knoxville, where Andrew was stationed during 1865. According to Wilson, this was a particularly happy time for the young Alexanders, and "their life in Knoxville was always a sunny memory . . ." (James B. Wilson, *The Life and Services of Brevet Brigadier General Andrew Jonathan Alexander*, pp. 92–93).

15. The remnants of the numerous Caddo people, originally inhabitants of eastern Texas, northern Louisiana, and southern Arkansas, were removed to Indian Territory in 1859 and settled on lands in the Leased District of the Choctaw Nation. The agency for the reservation was located on Leeper Creek about four miles from the present town of Fort Cobb, Oklahoma. Wright, *Guide to the Indian Tribes*, p. 51.

16. Fort Cobb was established in 1859 on the Washita River west of what is now Anadarko, Oklahoma. As Eveline notes, the post was abandoned in 1861. It was later briefly reactivated in 1868–1869. See Muriel H. Wright, "A History of Fort Cobb," *Chronicles of Oklahoma* 34 (Spring, 1956) : 53–71.

CHAPTER III

1. As Eveline notes later in her journal, Harwood eventually made his way back to Fort Smith and later rejoined his unit at Fort Union. For a fuller discussion of Harwood's ordeal, see George H. Shirk, ed., "The Lost Colonel," *Chronicles of Oklahoma* 35 (Summer, 1957) : 180–182, 191–193.

2. The Antelope Hills, a series of six irregular peaks on the South Canadian River in present Roger Mills County, Oklahoma, were a famous landmark for travelers on the Fort Smith–Santa Fe road. The description of this area given by Lieutenant Whipple during his 1853 reconnaissance is an interesting comparison to Evy's comments: " . . . the antelope hills . . . are composed of sandstones cemented with lime, and are of the mesa form. They are about a hundred and twenty-five feet high. . . . The route today through the Antelope hills, over prairies, and across ravines, has been dry and sandy. The scanty grass appeared of an earthy hue, relieved only by red gullies and occasional ravines, showing the foliage of stunted trees. A few pools of water were seen. But the valley of the Canadian, near camp [camp 36], displays green grass and patches of wood. The river is deeper and less muddy than before" (quoted in Grant Foreman, ed., *A Pathfinder in the Southwest: The Itinerary of Lieutenant A. W. Whipple*, pp. 76–77).

3. This "souvenir" scalp subsequently had a rather interesting history. On her arrival in New Mexico, Evy wrote her sister: "My dear sister, during my journey I was so fortunate as to find not only the scalp George commissioned me to procure him, but the 'war hoop' you had set your heart upon. As was quite natural I found them together. The 'hoop' was of bamboo with buckskin thongs attached to it, and the scalp was fastened within it by strings of sinew. But unfortunately it was left one

day where the pups found it, and they pulled the scalp out of the hoop and ran off with the latter. I rescued the scalp but the 'war-hoop' was among the missing. In my journal (part of which I sent home by mail this morning) you will find the particulars of the discovery of the scalp on the Antelope hills" (Eveline Alexander to her sister, Mary W. Martin, August 16, 1866, Booher Collection).

As to the reluctant Buffalo Hump, there seem to have been several Comanche chiefs known by that name. The one referred to by Eveline was probably "Pochanaw-quoip, called Buffalo Hump or Bull Hump by the whites," who was the "third ranking chief of the Penateka Comanches from about 1866–74" and "a raider and a troublemaker" (Wilbur S. Nye, *Plains Indian Raiders: The Final Phases of Warfare from the Arkansas to the Red River*, p. 236. See also, W. P. Webb and H. Bailey Carroll, eds., *The Handbook of Texas*, I, 241).

4. Max was one of Alexander's favorite mounts "who fell at Columbus, Georgia" (James B. Wilson, ed., *The Life and Services of Brevet Brigadier General Andrew Jonathan Alexander*, p. 10).

5. Like many other Anglos, Evy tended to overestimate Indian strength. The Comanches were by no means "the most numerous of any of the Indian tribes." There were probably no more than three thousand Comanches in all of the bands in 1866, but their great mobility and hit-and-run guerrilla tactics often led whites to believe the Comanches to be more numerous than they actually were. For example, one Texas observer reported twenty thousand Comanche tribesmen in Texas in 1859, while the U.S. Indian agent, Jesse Stem, estimated the actual number as closer to nineteen hundred. Muriel Wright, *Guide to the Indian Tribes of Oklahoma*, p. 119.

The Comanches were frequently hostile during this period. Despite a treaty negotiated between the United States and several Comanche bands in October, 1865, the failure of the government to live up to the terms of the agreement led to renewed warfare between Comanches and Anglos which continued off and on throughout the 1860's and 1870's. See Ernest Wallace and E. Adamson Hoebel, *The Comanches: Lords of the South Plains*, pp. 285–310, for a good summary of the Comanche wars.

6. In addition to the version given by Mrs. Alexander, there are several other theories about how the Staked Plain got its name. Although the term comes from the Spanish *Llano Estacado*, and *llano* means "plain," *estacado* can be translated as "staked," "palisaded," or even "stockaded." In fact, the original Spanish term may not have been *estacado* but rather *destacado*, "elevated or raised." For a fuller discussion, see Webb and Carroll, *Handbook of Texas*, II, 70.

7. The crossing was made in the vicinity of Adobe Walls, northeast of present-day Borger, Texas.

8. This route was laid out by lieutenants James W. Abert and William G. Peck of the U.S. Army Corps of Topographical Engineers. They made two reconnaissance trips in the area, the first in 1845 and the second in 1848. The portion of the route Evy refers to left the Canadian near Bluff Creek and proceeded northwest to Utah (or Ute) Creek and the

Santa Fe road. See W. Turrentine Jackson, *Wagon Roads West: A Study of Federal Road Surveys and Construction in the Trans-Mississippi West, 1846–1869*, pp. 107–108; and William H. Goetzmann, *Army Exploration in the American West, 1803–1863*, pp. 123–127, 144–149.

9. Eveline is misinformed, of course, about the arboreal characteristics of New Mexico. In addition to cottonwoods and evergreens, many other trees are abundant in the area.

10. Evy's misnaming of the river is not unusual for the time. During the early days of Anglo exploration in the West, the two rivers were frequently mistaken. In 1820 Major Stephen H. Long descended the Canadian River thinking he was on the Red and thus, as Goetzmann points out, "must be given credit for changing the ideas of map makers concerning the river systems of the southwest plains" (Goetzmann, *Army Exploration in the American West*, p. 43).

11. Fort Bascom was one of several posts established after the Civil War to help control the Comanches, Kiowas, and Apaches in the Canadian River and Red River regions. Located on the Canadian about twelve miles north of present Tucumcari, the post was in active operation from 1863 to 1870. Alexander commanded briefly at Bascom in early 1867. See James M. Foster, Jr., "Fort Bascom, New Mexico," *New Mexico Historical Review* 35 (January, 1960) : 30–62; and F. L. Crocchiola [F. Stanley], *Fort Bascom, Comanche-Kiowa Barrier*.

12. Dr. De Weisse's name does not appear on any of the lists of army officers, regular or volunteer, for this period. It may be that he was a contract surgeon instead of a military man. He evidently served only briefly at Bascom.

13. The regiment referred to is the First New Mexico Volunteers (later reorganized as the First New Mexico Cavalry), formed during the Civil War to help protect the territory as regular troops were withdrawn to battlefields in the East. In 1861 Carson replaced the original commander, Ceran St. Vrain, who resigned due to ill health. The volunteers served throughout the war, first against Sibley's Confederates and later in operations against the Indians in New Mexico and Arizona and as garrison troops for federal posts throughout the New Mexico Territory. Although the volunteers were severely criticized by many regular army officers, they rendered valuable service. The regiment remained on active duty until the fall of 1866, when the return of federal troops made it possible to release the volunteers. The last of the New Mexican companies served at Fort Garland until they were mustered out in 1867. See Ralph E. Twitchell, *The Leading Facts of New Mexican History*, II, 414, note 340; and F. L. Crocchiola [F. Stanley], *The Civil War in New Mexico*, pp. 387–399. Crocchiola's book includes a complete list of the New Mexican volunteers, who, contrary to Mrs. Alexander's statement, included a number of Mexican officers.

14. The command was still on the Canadian River. As discussed in note 10 above, the two rivers were frequently confused, and Eveline made a common error in misnaming the stream.

15. Mrs. Alexander obviously knew little more about Negroes than

she did about Indians. It is interesting to note that although the famous black woman Harriet Tubman lived in Auburn, not far from Willowbrook, neither Evy nor any other family member mentions her in their published works. Although Andrew's mother emancipated her slaves before the Civil War, the Alexanders had been slaveowners, and the Martins would appear to have been Unionist but not abolitionist.

16. Eveline is referring to a painting by the German-born artist Albert Bierstadt, a popular landscape painter of the period. In 1858 Bierstadt made a tour of the American West, and some of his best-known canvases are of Rocky Mountain scenes. The picture Evy recalled was probably "Thunderstorm in the Rocky Mountains," painted by Bierstadt about 1860.

17. Established in 1851 about eight miles north of the present town of Watrous, New Mexico, Fort Union became the center of operations and supply for the entire New Mexico Territory during the post–Civil War period. The fort complex included three installations: the post itself, laid out to accommodate four companies of cavalry, infantry, or a combination of both; a quartermaster depot; and an ordnance depot. Most troops arriving in New Mexico reported to Fort Union for assignment and often returned to the fort between stations. The Alexanders were at Union several times, and Andrew served as commander there from September, 1873, to July, 1874. Publications on the post include Robert M. Utley, "Fort Union and the Santa Fe Trail," *New Mexico Historical Review* 36 (January, 1961): 36–48; Chris Emmett, *Fort Union and the Winning of the Southwest*; F. L. Crocchiola [F. Stanley], *Fort Union*; and the excellent monograph by Robert M. Utley, *Fort Union National Monument, New Mexico*.

18. Barclay's Fort, at the junction of the Mora and Sapello rivers, was not a government installation but a private trading post built in 1848 by Alexander Barclay and his partner, Joseph Doyle. The fort included a large square enclosure with high walls and a heavy gate which served as a camping place for travelers. See Thomas M. Pearce, ed., *New Mexico Place Names: A Geographical Dictionary*, p. 57; Harvey Lewis Carter, *'Dear Old Kit': The Historical Christopher Carson*, p. 126, note 257; and Kenyon Riddle, *Records and Maps of the Old Santa Fe Trail*, pp. 122–140, which also includes a sketch map of the fort.

CHAPTER IV

1. Lydia Lane recalled the accident in her memoirs and reported that the driver went to sleep and the mules ran away, upsetting the ambulance. "The poor little woman," she noted of Mrs. Casey, "was found to be in great agony, and was lifted with difficulty. . . . Several ribs were broken, and she was badly bruised and sprained. . . . It was many months before she was able to walk about" (Lydia Spencer Lane, *I Married A Soldier; Or, Old Days in the Army*, pp. 133–134).

2. Another of the posts established to strengthen the southwestern frontier defense system, Fort Sumner was located on the Pecos River near the present town of the same name. Its principal mission was to

guard the Navajos and Mescalero Apaches confined at Bosque Redondo. The fort was abandoned in 1868 when the Navajos were allowed to return to their homes. See Charles Amsden, "The Navajo Exile at Bosque Redondo," *New Mexico Historical Review* 7 (January, 1933): 31–50; and James D. Shinkle, *Fort Sumner and the Bosque Redondo Indian Reservation.*

3. The reference here is to Andrew's brother, George Alexander, and his wife, Mary. "Compelled by ill health to seek a drier climate," George Alexander made his home in New Mexico for many years before his death in 1866. According to Wilson, " . . . his memory is still cherished by the early settlers of that wild country, who appreciated the purity and unselfishness of his character, as well as his reckless courage" (James B. Wilson, *The Life and Services of Brevet Brigadier General Andrew Jonathan Alexander,* p. 14).

4. Captain (and Brevet Lieutenant Colonel) William B. Lane, also of the Third Cavalry, and his wife arrived at Fort Union from Fort Leavenworth, Kansas, in the summer of 1866. Like Eveline, Lydia Lane loved New Mexico and wrote a book, previously cited, about her experiences. Although Mrs. Lane was older than Evy, they might have become good friends, since they had similar interests and backgrounds. However, they were never stationed at the same post at the same time. From Union, Lane was assigned to command at Fort Marcy at Santa Fe, where he served until January, 1867, when he returned to Fort Union.

5. Fort Craig was established in 1854 on the Rio Grande south of Socorro, New Mexico, as a protection against Apache raiders. It was abandoned in 1884. See F. L. Crocchiola [F. Stanley], *Fort Craig*; and Francis Paul Prucha, *A Guide to the Military Posts of the United States, 1789–1895,* p. 68.

6. Rayado Ranch was established in 1848 by Lucien Maxwell in the "fertile, well-watered valley of Rayado Creek near where the Taos trail left the main Santa Fe road." The ranch was west of present-day Springer. Maxwell and Kit Carson jointly engaged in a sheepraising business at Rayado, where Maxwell also developed extensive farming operations, furnishing forage for the army at Fort Union as well as other produce for sale. Jesús Abreu, a kinsman to Mrs. Maxwell, arrived at Rayado about 1857 and built a large home on the plaza next to Maxwell's. See Lawrence R. Murphy, "Rayado: Pioneer Settlement in Northeastern New Mexico, 1848–1857," *New Mexico Historical Review* 46 (January, 1971): 37–52; F. L. Crocchiola [F. Stanley], *Fort Union,* pp. 2–12; and Jim B. Pearson, *The Maxwell Land Grant,* pp. 10–11.

7. Rayado suffered several Indian attacks during the 1850's and 1860's. As a result, the army stationed troops there for a time. Of the reported raids, the one which conforms most closely to that described by Eveline was an attack by a reported "six hundred Apaches" in 1850. Murphy, "Rayado," p. 50. Whether Comanches or Apaches, however, the report of a war party of five to six hundred is undoubtedly an exaggeration. Indians in the area, and particularly the Comanches and Apaches, usually raided in small parties of no more than twenty. Furthermore,

Indians comprehended cannon well enough—at least well enough not to charge a heavily fortified position defended by artillery.

8. The Raton Mountains form part of a long range which divides northeastern New Mexico from Colorado. The Mountain Branch or Bent's Fort Cut-off of the Santa Fe Trail came from Trinidad over the Raton Pass along a road described as "extremely arduous and severe" (Kenyon Riddle, *Records and Maps of the Old Santa Fe Trail*, pp. 86–88).

9. Fishers Peak, located in the Raton Mountains, formed the northeastern corner of the Maxwell land grant and was a well-known local landmark. Fishers Peak was a great favorite of Lydia Lane, who noted: "Our tents were pitched in full view of Fisher's Peak in 1866, and we remained a day in the pretty camp. A soldier drew a picture of it for one of the children. . . . and I have a feeling of homesickness when I look at my picture" (Lane, *I Married A Soldier*, p. 137).

The Spanish Peaks, southwest of present-day Walsenburg, were also famous landmarks in the southern Colorado area. Called by the Indians *Huajatolla*, "breasts of the world," they were held in great awe by the Utes. Many legends and stories were associated with the peaks, including tales of lost gold mines and buried treasure. Federal Writers Project, *Colorado: A Guide to the Highest State*, pp. 374–375.

10. Evy is probably referring to the tollroad built by "Uncle Dick" Wootton in 1866 from Trinidad to the Canadian River in New Mexico. Riddle, *Records and Maps of the Old Santa Fe Trail*, pp. 88–89. Before the construction of Wootton's road, the Raton Pass was considered one of the most perilous stretches of the Santa Fe Trail for wheeled vehicles. For example, in 1846 it took the Magoffin party five days to travel through the pass. Stella M. Drumm, ed., *Down the Santa Fe Trail and into Mexico: The Diary of Susan Shelby Magoffin, 1846–1847*, pp. 79–80.

11. Although the site of Trinidad had been an Indian camp and a frequent stopping place on the Santa Fe Trail, no permanent settlement was located there until 1859. Later, the town became a center for the surrounding ranches and farms. In 1866, when Las Animas County was created, Trinidad was named as the county seat. The town was located on the Purgatoire River, originally named by the Spaniards El Río de las Ánimas Perdidas en Purgatorio (River of Souls Lost in Purgatory). Federal Writers' Project, *Colorado*, pp. 191–194. The Purgatoire was referred to by several different names, all variations of the French or Spanish spellings. Evy's "Purgatory" is an accurate translation, but it was probably used less commonly by the Anglos than the phonetic rendering of the French, "Picketwire."

12. Ceran de Hault de Lassus de St. Vrain was a well-known trader, merchant, and rancher. St. Vrain came to New Mexico in the 1820's, took Mexican citizenship, and with Cornelio Vigil secured a large land grant in the Huerfano, Apishapa, and Purgatoire valleys, in what is now southeastern Colorado. In 1854 and again in 1861 St. Vrain served as colonel of volunteers. His intimate knowledge of the country and his military experience made it possible for him to give expert advice on the location of Fort Stevens. See *Dictionary of American Biography*, XVI, 305–306;

and Harold H. Dunham, "Ceran St. Vrain," in *The Mountain Men and the Fur Trade of the Far West*, ed. LeRoy R. Hafen, V, 297–316. Enos was a regular army officer attached to the quartermaster's department. The ranch referred to was Colonel J. M. Francisco's residence on the Cuchara River.

CHAPTER V

1. No doubt because of its brief existence there is little information available on Fort Stevens, and it is rarely included on lists of U.S. forts and posts. As related here, it was located at the foot of the Spanish Peaks, southwest of present Walsenburg, Colorado. A short article in *Colorado Magazine* 43 (Fall, 1966): 303–307, consists principally of reprints of the general orders relating to the establishment of the fort, and there are a few brief notices in the *Santa Fe Weekly Gazette* (September 8, 1866, p. 2; September 29, 1866, p. 2) relating to the post. Aside from these sources and the official army records, however, Eveline's diary is probably the only extant description and history of Fort Stevens. The garrison for Fort Stevens consisted of G Company, Third Cavalry; companies F and H, Fifty-seventh Colored Infantry; officers Alexander, Lieutenant Mulford, and Lieutenant Carroll (who served as quartermaster and commissary officer, respectively); and surgeon Dr. Lee. Eveline Alexander to her sister, Lylie, August 22, 1866, Booher Collection; *Santa Fe Weekly Gazette*, September 29, 1866, p. 2.

2. Fort Garland, located in the San Luis Valley at the site of the modern town of San Luis, was at that time garrisoned by companies F and G of the First New Mexico Cavalry, one company of the First Volunteer California Infantry, and one company of the Thirteenth Missouri Cavalry. As federal forces returned to the frontier, the volunteer troops were gradually mustered out of service and replaced by regulars. During his inspection tour of 1866, General Sherman insisted that the volunteers be dismissed as quickly as possible and "the military establishment brought down to the regular army only" (Robert G. Athearn, *William Tecumseh Sherman and the Settlement of the West*, pp. 83–84). See also Gene M. Gressley, ed., "Report on Ft. Garland Made by Christopher (Kit) Carson to Major Roger James, June 10, 1866," *Colorado Magazine* 32 (July, 1955): 215–224.

3. This was a favorite nineteenth-century parlor game based, as the name implies, on Shakespearean quotations. There are several modern variations of the game, which was evidently similar to charades.

4. This rather oblique reference seems to concern mutual friends. "Marion" is probably Marion Sands, a girlhood friend of Eveline's. In a letter to her mother written from Washington in 1863, Eveline mentions a Colonel Dutton and the fact that "Marion Sands expects to be married the 9th of June, and wants me to be one of her bridesmaids" (Eveline Alexander to her mother, May 1, 1863, Booher Collection). Eveline's list of letters sent and received from 1866 includes "Marion Sands," and for 1867, "Marion Dutton." See also Edward S. Martin, *Some Account of Family Stocks Involved in Life at Willowbrook*, p. 77.

5. In 1866, General Sherman, as commander of the Military Division of the Missouri (which included the entire western United States from the Mississippi River to the Rockies) set out on a tour to assess the problems of patrolling the vast area, to investigate the "Indian problem," and to inspect wagon and railroad routes. Leaving Omaha in August, Sherman and his party proceeded by train to Fort Kearney, Nebraska, and then by ambulance westward to Fort Laramie and southward to Denver and Fort Garland. The trip, including the inspection of Fort Garland, is discussed in detail in Athearn, *William Tecumseh Sherman*, pp. 59–97.

During Sherman's stay at Fort Stevens, Eveline wrote, "He took a great deal of interest in pointing out to me on the map the position of the different new posts, and the boundaries of the four departments under his command . . . writing out on the margin of my Atlas the different territories each comprised and marking out the lines of the projected railroads west of the Mississippi. I found I had unconsciously hit upon one of the General's hobbies; he told me he spent hours looking over the maps of this western country. . . . He was much interested in 'Humbolt's [*sic*] New Spain,' which he found in my library, and carried it off to his tent saying he 'must sit up and read it tonight' " (Eveline Alexander to her mother, September 23, 1866, Booher Collection).

6. Sherman's visit to Fort Stevens, largely reconstructed from Eveline's letters, is detailed in James B. Wilson, *The Life and Services of Brevet Brigadier General Andrew Jonathan Alexander*, pp. 95–96. Wilson also reprints a letter from Sherman to Eveline, dated April 19, 1885, which reads in part: "I shall ever remember him [Alexander] and you when I sought refuge in your camp at Spanish Peaks . . . and when you both escorted me to Francisco's Ranch in a driving snow-storm" (ibid., p. 108).

7. Again, this family reference relates to Andrew's sister Apolline Alexander Blair. "Midge" may have been a nickname for Andrew's sister Mira Mariamne (Mrs. Franklin A. Dick of Philadelphia); Andrew was probably the Blair's oldest son, Andrew Alexander Blair; and Jim was probably another son, James Lawrence Blair. See "Blair Genealogy," in William Ernest Smith, *The Francis Preston Blair Family in Politics*.

8. This memorable event at Willowbrook is mentioned in Martin, *Life at Willowbrook*, p. 65, and detailed by Mrs. Cornelia Williams Martin in *The Old Home*, II, 35–36, as follows: "Mr. Seward, then Secretary of State, after the accession of the Vice-President to the Presidency, invited Mr. Johnson and the officers of his Cabinet and many of the distinguished men of that period to accompany him to his home at Auburn. . . . The company included President Johnson and many of the members of his Cabinet, among whom were Secretary Seward and Secretary Wells, the heroes of the War of the Rebellion, General Grant, Admiral Farragut, and other distinguished officers of the army and navy, including General Custer and General Fullerton. They were hospitably received by the citizens of Auburn, who gave them a dinner, which at Mr. Seward's suggestion, was served in the grove at the lake shore."

9. The reference is to Eveline's sister, Eliza Williams, usually called

Lylie or Lily, who married Grenville Tremain (incorrectly spelled "Tremaine" by Eveline), a college friend of the Martin boys, in October, 1868. Martin, *Life at Willowbrook*, pp. 67, 86.

The verse Eveline quotes in the entry for September 27 is from a song, "Little Doves," of which Andrew was quite fond. Eveline Alexander to her sister, Lily [Lylie], August 22, 1866, Booher Collection.

The term *no spondulix* was slang for "no money."

10. Keneatze, Kanneatche, or Ka-ni-ache (One Who Was Taken Down) was the leader of the Mohuache band of Utes. At one time Keneatze was a close friend of Kit Carson and served as scout for the doughty old frontiersman. However, as settlers moved into the area and land and buffalo became scarce, Keneatze became increasingly hostile and suspicious of all whites, including Carson. In 1863 Keneatze refused to sign an agreement to establish a new Ute reservation west of the Continental Divide and thereafter became known as a troublemaker and the leader of the dissident faction among the Utes. Wilson Rockwell, *The Utes, a Forgotten People*, p. 91; Mrs. Hal Russell, "Memoirs of Marian Russell," *Colorado Magazine* 21 (March, 1944) : 62. For a highly sympathetic view of Keneatze and a detailed account of the subsequent hostilities, see Morris F. Taylor, "Ka-ni-ache," *Colorado Magazine* 43 (Fall, 1966) : 275–302; and 44 (Spring, 1967) : 139–161.

11. This skirmish, although seemingly of a minor nature, caused a great uproar in northern New Mexico and southern Colorado. There are so many different, and frequent garbled, versions of the action that it is hard to understand how one minor incident could cause so much dissent and misunderstanding. Actually, the brief outbreak and the raid on Fort Stevens climaxed a series of incidents between Keneatze's Mohuache Utes and the army and the settlers in the San Luis Valley in which several people, including a Ute, were killed. Although Alexander was acting within the framework of his orders from General Carleton, many people, possibly including Carson, believed he had acted precipitously, while others thought his actions more than justified. Whatever the truth of this, as a result of the "battle" government authorities launched a full-scale investigation of the Utes' complaints, and an agreement between the Utes and the government was reached. Alexander was commended for his action by General Winfield Scott Hancock (see the letter of commendation printed in Wilson, *Life and Services*, pp. 98–99), and the incident passed into history. However, this was not Alexander's last "run-in" with Keneatze. In 1873, when Alexander was commanding Fort Garland, there was again trouble with Keneatze's band, and Alexander took troops out from the post to quell the disturbance. Taylor, "Ka-ni-ache," *Colorado Magazine* 44: 156–157.

On the background of the 1866 uprising, see Taylor, "Ka-ni-ache," *Colorado Magazine* 43:292–298; and Lawrence R. Murphy, *Philmont: A History of New Mexico's Cimarron County*, pp. 79–82. On the reaction of the settlers, see Russell, "Memoirs of Marian Russell," *Colorado Magazine* 21:62–63. (Mrs. Russell locates the battle "at the head of Longs Canyon . . . on the old George Thompson ranch") ; *Daily Rocky Mountain News*, October 11, 1866, p. 4, and October 27, 1866, p. 2; and *Santa Fe*

New Mexican, November 3, 1866, p. 2, and December 1, 1866, p. 1. Eve-line's version, as expected, conforms closely to that found in the official records, including Records of Fort Garland, Letters Sent, June, 1866–July, 1869, Record Group 98, National Archives, Washington, D.C., as cited in Taylor, "Ka-ni-ache"; and Superintendency of New Mexico, Letters Received, Office of Indian Affairs, 1866–1867, Record Group 75, National Archives, Washington, D.C.

Although the engagement was a minor one, it was officially included among the actions fought by the Third Cavalry, and the dead trooper, Louis Brickson, was listed among the regiment's casualties. See Ralph C. Deibert, *A History of the Third United States Cavalry,* pp. 24, 140; and Francis B. Heitman, *Historical Register and Dictionary of the United States Army,* II, 354, 427.

12. Badito was a small settlement at the entrance to the Huerfano Valley. Federal Writers' Project, *Colorado,* p. 350.

13. Evy seems quite calm and matter-of-fact in reporting these events, including the raid on Fort Stevens. However, her handwriting betrays her concern and agitation. The writing in this part of the journal is hurried, scratchy, and almost illegible, suggesting that she was more apprehensive or excited than her words seem to indicate. However, since she was sending copies of the diary home, she probably did not want to alarm her family. In letters written at the time, she carefully played down the danger. "You must not feel anxious about us in regard to the Indians," she wrote her mother. "They are all at peace now; and considerably more polite than they have been for sometime. Besides in a fort one is always safe, for they have never been known to attack a fort. That report of a garrison being murdered in Arizona was all a canard. I was asking Sherman when he was here if there was any truth in it and he said 'no indeed.' I am not in the least afraid of the Indians" (Eveline Alexander to her mother, October 16, 1866, Booher Collection).

14. Fort Garland was established in June, 1858, and garrisoned by troops from the abandoned Fort Massachusetts to protect settlers in the San Luis Valley from attacks by Utes and Apaches. Abandoned in November, 1883, the post fell into disrepair until it was acquired in 1950 by the State of Colorado and restored as a state historical monument. See John H. Nankivell, "Fort Garland, Colorado," *Colorado Magazine* 16 (January, 1939): 13–27, for a history of the fort, including a picture of the Carson quarters occupied by the Alexanders. Gressley, "Report on Ft. Garland," gives a good account of the post at the time the Alexanders were stationed there in 1866. As noted above, Alexander again served at Garland, first in 1871 and again during 1872–1873. "Statement of the military service of Andrew J. Alexander," June 10, 1885, filed with Pension Application File #335-245, 3632 ACP 1887, Record Group 94, National Archives, Washington, D.C.

15. Although I have regularized her spelling, Evy usually wrote the word "Peublo." This spelling was not uncommon in the nineteenth century. See, for example, De Witt C. Peters, *The Life and Adventures of Kit Carson,* for the same spelling.

16. Stories of the Aztecs as the first inhabitants of the pueblos have

persisted since Spanish times. No less a renowned scientist than Alexander von Humboldt believed the Aztec theory and even specified their camping or stopping places on his maps. When the first Anglos arrived in New Mexico, they reinforced these legends: Josiah Gregg wove the story into his *Commerce of the Prairies*. Lieutenant William H. Emory, exploring the area with Kearny's army in 1846, noted the "Montezuma fires" and compared the ruined Pueblan villages with those "Aztec and Mayan civilizations . . . described by Prescott . . . and Stephens." Lieutenant Abert believed he saw a clear connection between the Acoma pueblos and the Aztec culture. William H. Goetzmann, *Army Exploration in the American West, 1803–1863*, pp. 135–136, 146–147. However, as Frederick W. Hodge's authoritative *Handbook of American Indians North of Mexico*, points out, "There is no ground whatever for the belief that any of the Southwestern pueblos or cliff villages are of Mexican origin" (I, 935). An excellent summary of the Montezuma legends can be found in Benjamin M. Read, "The Last Word on 'Montezuma,'" *New Mexico Historical Review* 1 (July, 1926) : 350–358.

17. This story bears a close resemblance to the teachings of the Paiute prophet, Wovoka, originator of the famous Ghost Dance religion. Although the legend, as reported by Eveline, predates the Ghost Dance cult by several years, the beliefs on which the religion was based had been in circulation long before they were popularized by Wovoka. See Henry F. Dobyns and R. C. Euler, *The Ghost Dance of 1889 among the Indians of Northwestern Arizona*, on the history and development of the Ghost Dance, and Marvin K. Opler, "The Southern Ute of Colorado," in *Acculturation in Seven American Indian Tribes*, ed. Ralph Linton, pp. 188–189, for an account of the religion among the southern Utes.

18. Evy's relations with "Old Kit" seem to have been rather unusual. Ordinarily Carson was shy around women, particularly the army wives. Lydia Lane recalled, for example: "Once, when going from Santa Fe to Fort Union, no less a person than Kit Carson . . . made one of the party. To see the quiet, reticent man, you never would dream that he was the hero of so many romances. I believe he would rather have faced a whole tribe of hostile Indians than one woman, he was so diffident . . . (Lydia Spencer Lane, *I Married A Soldier; Or, Old Days in the Army*, p. 148).

Marian Russell, who had known Carson since her girlhood, noted: "I distinctly recall Kit Carson. . . . He was exceedingly kind and courteous to me, a man short of stature, slow of speech and sparing in conversation, though ever solicitous of our comfort" (Albert W. Thompson, "Kit Carson's Camp Nichols in No Man's Land," *Colorado Magazine* 11 (September, 1934) : 184).

Even Andrew commented on Carson's relationship to Eveline. As she wrote in a letter home: "If I could only have spent the winter with old Kit, by spring I should have been ready to 'write a book.' Andrew says he took an uncommon fancy to me, and talked to me more freely than to him or any other man" (Eveline Alexander to her mother, December 16, 1866, Booher Collection).

19. Usually called Ouray or U-ray by the Anglos, this leader of the Tabeguache Utes was also known as Oolay or Ulay. The son of a Ute

mother and a Jicarilla Apache father, Ouray was raised on a New Mexican ranch, where he learned to speak excellent Spanish and fair English. He later returned to his mother's people and quickly rose to a position of prominence. In 1863 Ouray was one of a delegation of Ute, Cheyenne, and Arapaho chiefs who visited Washington, and later that same year he was influential in getting many of the Ute bands to agree to a treaty negotiated with U.S. agents at Conejos. Throughout his life Ouray remained friendly with the U.S. government, often in opposition to his own people. According to Hodge, *Handbook of American Indians*, II, 175, "He is noted chiefly for his unwavering friendship for the whites, with whom he always kept faith and whose interests he protected as far as possible, even on trying occasions." See also Rockwell, *The Utes*, pp. 88–90; and Thomas F. Dawson, "Major Thompson, Chief Ouray, and the Utes," *Colorado Magazine* 7 (May, 1930): 113–122.

20. Eveline's description of the Ute camp makes an interesting comparison to that of another contemporary observer, General James F. Rusling, who made an inspection tour for the quartermaster general's office in 1866 and joined Sherman's party at Denver. Rusling attended the Ute council on September 21 and 22 at Fort Garland and reported as follows on the Ute camp there: " . . . a number of us walked over to the Indian village to return our calls. We found it to consist of perhaps three hundred wigwams, arranged pretty regularly in streets, and containing in all some twelve hundred souls. The wigwams or lodges were made of skins and hides, stretched over circularly inclined poles—rude originals evidently of our army Sibley tents—with an opening at the top for the smoke to escape through. At the door were planted their spears or lances and shields; inside on skins or blankets, the braves were fast asleep or playing cards . . . " (James F. Rusling, *Across America; Or, the Great West and the Pacific Coast*, pp. 116–117).

21. For all his reputation as an Indian fighter, Kit Carson had respect for his Indian foes. Unlike many Anglos, he believed they should be treated fairly and honestly, and several times he served as agent to various tribal groups. Carson seemed to have enjoyed a particularly close relationship with a number of Utes, frequently using them as scouts, and in 1868 he accompanied a Ute delegation to Washington to assist them in drawing up a treaty with the U.S. government. Harvey Lewis Carter, *'Dear Old Kit': The Historical Christopher Carson*, pp. 160–164, 170–174. See also Richard N. Ellis, ed., "Bent, Carson, and the Indians, 1865," *Colorado Magazine* 46 (Winter, 1969): 55–68.

Rusling noted the same friendliness between the Utes and Carson as did Eveline. Rusling, *Across America*, p. 137. The published literature on Carson is extensive, and no attempt has been made here to consult all of it. In addition to Edwin L. Sabin's classic studies *Kit Carson Days (1809–1868)* and *Kit Carson Days, 1809–1868: Adventures in the Path of Empire*, the best (and certainly the most balanced) source is Carter, *'Dear Old Kit.'* On Carson's relations with the Indians, Marshall D. Moody, "Kit Carson, Agent to the Indians in New Mexico, 1853–1861," *New Mexico Historical Review* 28 (January, 1953): 1–20, is helpful, as is Ellis, "Bent, Carson, and the Indians."

22. Stories of cannibalism among the survivors of Frémont's ill-fated fourth expedition, although never proven, have long persisted in the folklore of the Southwest. A good summary of the 1848–1849 disaster and a balanced assessment of the cannibalism charge is found in Allan Nevins, *Frémont, Pathmarker of the West*, pp. 343–372. As noted earlier, Eveline was somewhat naïve in her outlook and willing to accept the stories related by Carson and other westerners as fact. In regard to the charges against Frémont, she was probably particularly willing to believe what she was told, since Frémont and Alexander's brother-in-law, Frank Blair, Jr., were bitter enemies.

23. The reference here is to Lucien Maxwell's famous establishment at Cimarron. After leaving Rayado, Maxwell moved to the Cimarron River (the tributary of the Canadian, not the much larger Cimarron that flows to the Arkansas), where he built a new headquarters, including a lavish mansion "complete with servants, hardwood floors and silver service." Maxwell's ranch on the Cimarron, with its gristmill, corrals, stables, and other buildings, "became the hub of the Cimarron country" (Jim Berry Pearson, *The Maxwell Land Grant*, pp. 11–12). In 1862 the government negotiated a twenty-year lease with Maxwell for twelve hundred acres of land near the Cimarron as a reservation for the Utes and Jicarilla Apaches. William A. Keleher, *Maxwell Land Grant: A New Mexico Item*, pp. 46–47, 52–53.

24. General Rusling was also impressed by Ouray, and his description of the Ute chief is similar to Eveline's: "The head chief of the tribe, and the finest looking Indian we have yet seen, was Ooray. He was a medium sized, athletic looking man, of about forty, with as fine an eye and head, as you will see anywhere. Moreover, he was very neat and clean in his person, as if he believed in the saving virtues of soap and water . . . " (Rusling, *Across America*, p. 124).

25. In 1866 Congress authorized six regiments of Negro troops (two cavalry and four infantry regiments) as part of the regular peacetime army. Since the use of blacks as regular soldiers was considered something of an experiment, every effort was made to secure top-flight officers for the new units. All officers appointed to the units had to have at least two years of active field service and take a special examination before a board of officers appointed by the secretary of war. The Ninth, as Eveline notes, was commanded by Colonel Edward Hatch of Iowa, a highly respected officer with a brilliant Civil War record, and the other officers had equally distinguished reputations. Interestingly enough, George A. Custer was one of the men considered for a commission with the Ninth, a position he refused. See William H. Leckie, *The Buffalo Soldiers: A Narrative of the Negro Cavalry in the West*, pp. 6–8.

CHAPTER VI

1. Shawynoa was one of the subchiefs of the Tabegauche band of Utes. The name is spelled in various ways. Wilson Rockwell, *The Utes, a Forgotten People*, p. 91, gives the name as Shavano; James F. Rusling, *Across America; Or, the Great West and the Pacific Coast*, p. 124, says his name was Chi-chis-na-sau-no, abbreviated as Shauno; while M. Mor-

gan Estergreen, *Kit Carson: A Portrait in Courage*, p. 271, prefers Shawno and says he was one of the men sent to bring Keneatze to Fort Garland after the 1866 raid. (However, since Estergreen places the raid in the summer of 1867, a date evidently based on Bancroft's *History of Nevada, Colorado and Wyoming*, his account may not be too reliable.) Eveline changes the spelling later in the diary and refers to the Ute as Chief Chavenau.

2. Taos, an important early settlement and a center for the Rocky Mountain fur trade, was known by various names during its long history. During the Spanish period in New Mexico, settlers huddled together in small fortified communities called "plazas," which in New Mexico referred to a fortified place rather than a central square. The New Mexican plaza consisted of a series of contiguous houses built around a central open area which could be entered only by means of wide, fortified gates. Taos included four such plaza communities: Taos, Ranchos de Taos, Trampas, and Dixon. There was a similar plan in the settlement at Rayado, as Evy relates in her earlier description. On the plaza arrangement and early Taos, see David J. Weber, *The Taos Trappers: The Fur Trade in the Far Southwest, 1540–1846*, p. 4; and Bainbridge Bunting, *Taos Adobes: Spanish Colonial and Territorial Architecture of the Taos Valley*, p. 3.

The other two towns Eveline mentions were small villages on the road from Raton to Santa Fe. Costilla, at the southern end of the San Luis Valley just south of the Colorado–New Mexico line, was a trading point for ranchers along the Rio Costilla, which curves through the town. Arroyo Hondo, twelve miles northwest of Taos, was another "plaza" town consisting of three such communities settled in 1823. Thomas M. Pearce, ed., *New Mexico Place Names: A Geographical Dictionary*, pp. 11, 41; Federal Writers' Project, *New Mexico: A Guide to the Colorful State*, p. 286.

3. William LeBlanc, a French Canadian fur trapper, came to New Mexico about 1820. For a time LeBlanc worked for Bent, St. Vrain and Company, but later took a job as a carpenter at Simeon Turley's mill and distillery near Arroyo Hondo. As LeBlanc told Eveline, he was one of the men who escaped during the attack on Turley's mill during the 1847 revolt. He went north to the Arkansas River but later returned to New Mexico and settled at Arroyo Hondo. Jane Lecompte, "William LeBlanc," *The Mountain Men and the Fur Trade of the Far West*, ed. LeRoy R. Hafen, V, 171–172.

4. LeBlanc's story of the Frémont expedition and his role in the rescue of the survivors differs in several important details from the official reports and recollections of the expedition's members. Certainly LeBlanc's story in regard to Williams varies significantly from the account given by Williams' biographer, Alpheus H. Favour, in *Old Bill Williams, Mountain Man*, pp. 167–196. Whether LeBlanc was trying to impress Eveline or an old man's memory was faulty (LeBlanc was about sixty-two at the time the Alexanders visited with him) is hard to tell. LeBlanc's account can be checked against the reports of other participants in the affair reprinted in LeRoy R. Hafen and Ann Hafen, eds.,

Frémont's Fourth Expedition: A Documentary Account of the Disaster of 1848–1849. See also, note 22, chapter 5 above.

5. On the Taos revolt of 1847 LeBlanc seems more reliable. At least his story corresponds more exactly to other accounts of the incident, in which the Mexican and Indian population rose in revolt, murdered Governor Bent, and attacked various Anglo-American outposts, including Turley's Mill near Arroyo Hondo. There are numerous accounts of the revolt, but good summaries are available in Weber, *The Taos Trappers*, pp. 227–229; Ralph E. Twitchell, *Leading Facts of New Mexican History*, II, 228–261; and Warren A. Beck, *New Mexico: A History of Four Centuries*, pp. 134–138. LeBlanc was one of the members of the jury that tried the instigators of the revolt. See Francis T. Cheetham, "The First Term of the American Court in Taos, New Mexico," *New Mexico Historical Review* (hereafter cited as *NMHR*) 1 (January, 1926): 23–41.

Eveline is confused about the date of the revolt, which erupted in January, 1847, not 1848, as she states here. Later in the diary she correctly gives the date as 1847.

6. Teresina Bent Scheurich was Kit Carson's niece, and her husband, Aloys Scheurich, was an old New Mexico settler and a close friend and associate of Carson. For many years Mrs. Scheurich was a pillar of the Taos community and much interested in preserving its early history as well as that of her father, the murdered Governor Charles Bent, and her uncle. For a brief sketch of Mrs. Scheurich, see Blanche C. Grant, *When Old Trails Were New: The Story of Taos*, pp. 161–162, and various references to both Mrs. Scheurich and her husband in Estergreen, *Kit Carson*.

The decor of the Scheurich home and the use of "cigarettos" by the ladies of the household are both typical for the time and place. Weber notes in *The Taos Trappers*, p. 8, that many Americans were charmed by the New Mexican ladies' smoking habits. Certainly this was the opinion of young Lewis Garrard, who visited New Mexico in 1847 and commented: "Though smoking is repugnant to many ladies, it certainly does enhance the charms of the Mexican senoritas, who, with neatly rolled-up shucks between coral lips, perpetrate winning smiles, their magically brilliant eyes the meanwhile searching one's very soul . . ." (Lewis H. Garrard, *Wah-To-Yah and the Taos Trail*, p. 171).

Eveline's description of a New Mexican home is similar to that of Lydia Lane, who wrote: "There was seldom any furniture in the room; the dirt floor was neatly covered by a woollen carpet of black and white plaid, made by the Mexicans, which, though not very gay, looked tidy. . . . Around the walls were laid wool mattresses, neatly folded and covered with gay calico; these served as seats for the Mexicans. The small, narrow, wool-stuffed pillows were there also covered with red or pink calico, over which as drawn coarse lace, like a case, with wide lace ruffles on the ends . . . " (Lydia Spencer Lane, *I Married A Soldier; Or, Old Days in the Army*, p. 95).

7. Taos Pueblo, two and one-half miles from the town, consisted, as Eveline notes, of two parts separated by Taos Creek. Originally built

during the Pueblo IV period (ca. 1275–1598), additions were made during Pueblo V (after 1598). Bunting, *Taos Adobes*, p. 1. Descriptions by other Anglo observers of the period are similar to Eveline's. See, for example, Garrard, *Wah-To-Yah*, p. 188; Lansing B. Bloom, "The Rev. Hiram Walter Read, Baptist Missionary," *NMHR* 17 (April, 1942) : 126; and the much later but still similar description by the archeologist Edgar L. Hewett in Adolph F. Bandelier and Edgar L. Hewett, *Indians of the Rio Grande Valley*, p. 76.

8. This is a reference to the old mission church of San Gerónimo de Taos, destroyed by Colonel Sterling Price during the revolt of 1847. A new church was built after that date, and some of the paintings and other relics from the older structure were moved to the new building. The "caballero" described by Eveline does not represent Cortés, but rather the patron saint of Spain, Saint James. For a history of the Taos church, see George Kubler, *The Religious Architecture of New Mexico in the Colonial Period and Since the American Occupation*, pp. 113–114, 126–127. A full description of the old church, including a discussion of the paintings on buckskin, can be found in Eleanor B. Adams and Angélico Chávez, trans. and eds., *The Missions of New Mexico, 1776: A Description by Fray Francisco Atanasio Dominquez with Other Contemporary Documents*, pp. 101–113. A history of the Pueblo and its missions is Myra Ellen Jenkins, "Taos Pueblo and Its Neighbors, 1540–1847," *NMHR* 41 (April, 1966) : 85–114.

9. These *"estoffes"* or *estufas* (Spanish for stove) were underground Pueblan ceremonial chambers or *kivas*. Visits to these sites seem to have been a favorite pastime for Anglos. The Reverend Mr. Read also visited the kiva at Taos, which he described as ". . . rooms under ground, used for Council chambers. The entrance is by a small trap door and a perpendicular ladder. The chamber is about seven feet deep, circular, and some twenty feet in diameter" (Bloom, "The Rev. Hiram Walter Read," pp. 125–126). Read also recounts the story of the "Montezuma fires" in much the same detail as Evy. However, like other Montezuma stories, the perpetual fire legends were of European origin but perpetuated by the Pueblans in order to camouflage and guard Indian religious practices. See Charles H. Lange and Carroll L. Riley, eds., *The Southwestern Journals of Adolph F. Bandelier, 1880–1882*, p. 78, note 64; and Edward H. Spicer, *Cycles of Conquest: The Impact of Spain, Mexico, and the United States on the Indians of the Southwest, 1533–1960*, p. 165.

10. It is not certain just which ruins Eveline refers to here. There are a number of ancient sites in the vicinity of Taos, some of which have recently been excavated. However, her description is too sketchy to make positive identification possible. See Lange, *Southwestern Journals of Adolph F. Bandelier*, p. 357.

11. In a letter Eveline described her quarters at Union as follows: "We are most comfortably fixed here. Have three rooms, beautifully finished off, and a kitchen; a side hall separates ours from Colonel Marshall's rooms—in the same house. The house is built of adobe, and very warm. It was just completed this spring. Mr. and Mrs. Carroll have

one of our rooms at present, but they have just received orders to go to Albuquerque and leave in a few days" (Eveline Alexander to her mother, November 11, 1866, Booher Collection).

12. Eveline's phonetic spelling presents some problems in identifying persons of Indian or Spanish ancestry. She may be referring to the Mohuache subchief Ancotah or Ancantah, who, according to Morris F. Taylor, "Ka-ni-ache," *Colorado Magazine* 43 (Fall, 1966): 302, attended the council at Taos following the Ute raids of 1866. However, Taylor gives no indication that he replaced Keneatze.

13. The Pueblan "Elk Dance" described here is probably the Deer Dance, one of the favorite hunting dances of the Pueblos which is still performed today. For descriptions of the dance, see Bandelier and Hewett, *Indians of the Rio Grande Valley*, p. 55, and Elsie C. Parsons, *Pueblo Indian Religion*, II, 844–847.

14. Like the Montezuma legends, rumors of human sacrifice among the Pueblos were common during the nineteenth century but had no basis in fact. See Oliver La Farge with Arthur N. Morgan, *Santa Fe: The Autobiography of a Southwestern Town*, pp. 189–190, for a similar report and refutation.

15. Moqui is an old name for the Hopi. The name probably originated with the Spaniards. See John Francis Bannon, *The Spanish Borderlands Frontier, 1513–1821*, p. 18.

16. As explained above (note 25, chapter 5), the legislation establishing the first units of black regulars required all officers appointed to these commands to submit to a special examination. War Department Special Orders No. 561, November 10, 1866, directed a board of officers to meet at Santa Fe on December 10, 1866, to examine Alexander. The board convened on December 17, 1866, and found him "duly qualified by his Services during the War, and his soldierly ability to perform the duties of Major of the 9th U.S. Cavalry."

17. Tecolote, settled about 1824, was a busy trading point about thirty miles from Fort Union and ten miles from modern Las Vegas. During the 1860's it served as a forage and remount station for the army. In an excellent contemporary description, early Colorado settler Marian Russell writes: "Tecolote, like all Mexican towns consisted of low adobi [sic] houses and narrow crooked streets; yet it was thriving and prosperous. . . . The trading post at Tecolote was a meeting place for all the nomads of that desert land [and] it was very exciting when the freight trains pulled in" (Russell, "Memoirs of Marian Russell," *Colorado Magazine* 21 (March, 1944): 64–65). See also Pearce, *New Mexico Place Names*, p. 163.

Kozlowski's ranch was owned by a Martin or Andrew Kozlowski, a Polish immigrant and U.S. Army veteran. The ranch figured prominently in the battle of Glorieta Pass, March 26–28, 1862, as the Union Army camp. In addition to his ranching activities, Kozlowski also operated a store at Rowe on the Santa Fe Trail. According to one source, he is reputed to have "used timber from Pecos pueblo and mission ruins in building [his] ranch" (Lange, *The Journals of Adolph F. Bandelier*, pp. 411–412). See also Ray C. Colton, *The Civil War in the Western Territories: Arizona, Colorado, New Mexico, and Utah*, p. 50, note. 4.

Notes

159

18. Descriptions of Santa Fe at the time of the Alexanders' visit there may be found in Ralph Emerson Twitchell, *Old Santa Fe: The Story of New Mexico's Ancient Capital*, pp. 368–397; and James F. Meline, *Two Thousand Miles on Horseback: Santa Fe and Back*, pp. 151–157, 180–194.

As Eveline notes, Protestants were few in Santa Fe. The first Protestant denomination to make much progress there was the Baptists who, led by the Reverend Hiram W. Read, built a meeting hall on Grant Avenue near Griffin Street. According to a local newspaper, "This is the first and only protestant meeting-house erected in the territory of New Mexico. . . . It is a neat and comfortable adobe building, forty-one feet long, exclusive of a vestibule ten feet square and thirty-one feet wide. The finish is plain and substantial, with pews sufficient to accommodate about one hundred and fifty persons. The ceiling is supported by four square pillars, and the pulpit, in the modern platform style, is at the north end" (Twitchell, *Old Santa Fe*, p. 365, note 653). Erected in 1854, the building was sold to the Presbyterians in 1866 (ibid., p. 456). Just when the roof collapsed is not clear, but Meline, who also visited Santa Fe in 1866, noted that the building was "rather nice looking" despite "its fallen-in roof and nailed-up windows" (Meline, *Two Thousand Miles*, p. 192).

19. Pecos Church and Pueblo are among the most extensively explored, excavated, and studied of any of the New Mexican ruins. For information on the church, see Kubler, *Religious Architecture of New Mexico*, pp. 85–87, and on the Pueblo, the pioneering work of Alfred Vincent Kidder, *An Introduction to the Study of Southwestern Archaeology, with a Preliminary Account of the Excavations at Pecos*, pp. 61–139. Both Kidder and Kubler noted, as did Eveline, the use of materials from the church for building in the neighborhood of Pecos. However, Evy did not seem to realize that by carrying away even small pieces of "carved wood" and "a little Aztec image" she was adding to the destruction of the site. Pot hunting, or at least souvenir collecting, by tourists has changed remarkably little since 1866.

20. One cannot help but comment that had Eveline only known what would happen to the Seventh Cavalry nearly ten years later, she would probably have been happier to have had Keogh remain with the "hard-drinking" Fourth rather than join the more colorful Seventh.

21. Alexander briefly served as commander at Bascom, a post described by Marian Russell as ". . . a picturesque little place among low rolling foothills. Here the soldier's [sic] quarters, as at Ft. Union, were of log. They were arranged around a square parade ground, in the center of which stood the flag pole" (Russell, "Memoirs of Marian Russell," *Colorado Magazine* 21 [January, 1944]: 33–34). Since Bascom's location can hardly be described as "southeastern" in relation to New Mexico, one assumes that Eveline meant that the fort was located southeast of the main New Mexican settlements. A history and description of the fort, as noted above, is found in James M. Foster, Jr., "Fort Bascom, New Mexico," *NMHR* 35 (January, 1960): 30–62.

22. The expedition briefly traced here agrees with the account given in Foster, "Fort Bascom," pp. 39–40, based on the official army reports.

Foster seems to doubt Alexander's intention to allow the Navajos to escape, but Eveline's journal clarifies this point. Although still operating under General James Carleton's infamous orders to "kill any male Indian caught off the reservation," Alexander, like many other officers, disagreed with this policy. In his dealings with the Utes, the Navajos, and later with other western Indians, Alexander adopted an attitude of firmness but fairness. When he left the Verde district of Arizona in 1869, Alexander received a letter written on behalf of Antonio Azul, the Pima chief, thanking him for the "many kindnesses" the Pimas had received from him and expressing the tribe's sadness at his leaving. William Bichard to A. J. Alexander, quoted in James B. Wilson, *The Life and Services of Brevet Brigadier General Andrew Jonathan Alexander*, p. 102.

23. The Bosque Redondo Reservation near Fort Sumner, originally established for the Mescalero Apaches, became a center for the concentration of the Navajos after Carson's 1863–1864 campaign. Soon the area was overcrowded, administration was confused, crops failed, rations were inadequate, and conflicts between Navajos and Apaches were frequent. In 1865, as Eveline reports, the Apaches decamped, leaving behind only "nine sick and crippled" (*Report of the Commissioner of Indian Affairs for 1866*, quoted in C. L. Sonnichsen, *The Mescalero Apaches*, p. 119).

24. Evy's description of Bosque Redondo corresponds to other contemporary descriptions. According to one account: "The brackish water they drank brought dysentery . . . [and] the reservation, situated on the edge of a treeless expanse of prairie, quickly depleted fuel close at hand. Resources of cedar and mesquite retreated farther and farther . . . until Navajos were traveling twelve to twenty miles for mesquite root, which they carried 'upon their galled and lacerated backs' " (Lynn R. Bailey, *The Long Walk: A History of the Navajo Wars, 1846–68*, pp. 223–224). According to the same report, conditions in 1867 were so bad at the reservation that the "Navajos had to be forced to work at bayonet point . . ." (ibid, p. 223). On the history of the Navajos at Bosque Redondo, see also Lynn R. Bailey, *Bosque Redondo: An American Concentration Camp*; Lawrence C. Kelly, *Navajo Roundup: Selected Correspondence of Kit Carson's Expedition against the Navajo, 1863–1865*; Charles Amsden, "The Navajo Exile at Bosque Redondo," *NMHR* 8 (January, 1933): 31–50; and Frank D. Reeve, "The Federal Indian Policy in New Mexico, 1858–1880," *NMHR* 12 (July, 1937): 248–269; and 13 (January, 1938): 14–49.

Although it is not stressed in this part of the journal, Eveline became increasingly concerned about the plight of the Navajo people. She prepared an article about them for the *New York Observer* and with her mother attempted to set up an organization to provide missionaries and other workers for the reservation. Eveline Alexander to her mother, February 22, 1867, and an undated letter, both in the Booher Collection.

25. Fort Wingate was located in northwestern New Mexico near present-day Gallup. See Frank McNitt, "Old Fort Wingate," *El Palacio* 79 (1972): 30-36.

CHAPTER VII

1. During this period in New Mexican history, a number of adventurers, ambitious politicians, and speculators crowded into the territory. Both the U.S. Army and the Indian Service found themselves the victims of unscrupulous persons intent upon increasing their own personal power and wealth through supplying government contracts. Charges of chicanery, fraud, and outright theft among the government suppliers were frequent, and there were numerous complaints and examples of short measures and inferior goods furnished at exorbitant prices. In the case of beef supplies, for example, it was charged that the animals sold to the army and Indian reservations were "bulls, poor stags and shelly cows . . . not more than fit for wolf bait." Grant, as secretary of war, was greatly concerned with the rations for troops and for the Indians, and this, undoubtedly, was the reason for his affirmative response to Alexander's suggestion for the inspection. On the operation of frauds in government contracts, see, for example, Howard R. Lamar, *The Far Southwest, 1846–1912: A Territorial History*, pp. 136–159; and William A. Keleher, *Turmoil in New Mexico, 1846–1868*, pp. 349–368.

2. Eveline refers here to the troopers wounded during the action against the Utes in Colorado.

3. Fort Stanton, on the Rio Bonito in Lincoln County, was established in 1855, partially destroyed during the Civil War, and rebuilt in 1868 to aid in control of the Mescalero and White Mountain Apaches. Fort Bliss, at El Paso, Texas, established in 1849, became an important center for military activities along the Rio Grande and the Texas–New Mexico border. See Robert W. Frazer, *Forts of the West: Military Forts and Presidios and Posts Commonly Called Forts West of the Mississippi River to 1898*, pp. 103–104, 143–144; and Francis Paul Prucha, *A Guide to the Military Posts of the United States, 1789–1895*, pp. 61, 109.

4. Almost everyone stationed at Fort Union complained of the winds. Lydia Lane recalled that the post was continually swept by winds that "howled and shrieked . . . doing everything wind ever does in the way of making a noise" (Lane, *I Married A Soldier; Or, Old Days in the Army*, p. 151).

5. Evidently Eveline's earlier plans to live at Santa Fe changed, and instead she determined to remain at Fort Union. Captain William R. Shoemaker, with whom she was staying, was something of an institution at Fort Union. He had been military storekeeper and keeper of ordnance there since 1851. When he retired in 1882, he asked and was given permission to retain his quarters at the arsenal. See Chris Emmett, *Fort Union and the Winning of the Southwest*, p. 395; and Robert M. Utley, *Fort Union National Monument, New Mexico*, p. 52, for sketches of Shoemaker.

6. Hatch and the Ninth Cavalry left New Orleans for Texas during the spring of 1867. Two companies were stationed at Brownsville, while the remainder of the regiment occupied forts Stockton and Davis. Contrary to what Eveline implies, however, the regiment was by no means fully trained or equipped, and it suffered many difficulties (including a

mutiny) during its first months in Texas. William H. Leckie, *The Buffalo Soldiers: A Narrative of the Negro Cavalry in the West*, pp. 11–12. Alexander never joined the Ninth Cavalry, but instead, after making his report to Grant in Washington, was assigned to the Eighth Cavalry and sent to Fort McDowell, Arizona, as post commander.

7. The practice of selling or auctioning excess goods and household effects was common among officers' families stationed in the West. Moving allowances were minimal, and the wives soon learned to "travel light." Lydia Lane discusses several sales of household goods before her various moves, and another army wife, Ellen McGowan Biddle, recalled: "Whenever an officer left the Territory it was the practice to have an auction, selling off everything he did not care to keep. These auctions were a great institution. They enabled the settlers to buy furniture and other things at a fair price" (Ellen McGowan Biddle, *Reminiscences of a Soldier's Wife*, pp. 172–173).

8. Eveline evidently thought she was pregnant. Either she miscarried or else she was mistaken. The Alexander's first child, a daughter, was born in Arizona in July, 1868.

Bibliography

IN addition to Mrs. Alexander's manuscript diary in the Bancroft Library of the University of California at Berkeley, I have quoted excerpts from her letters in the private collection of Mr. and Mrs. Edward E. Booher, Cranbury, New Jersey. I have also consulted materials in the National Archives, Washington, D.C. (record groups 75, 94, 98, and 393) and the Texas State Archives, Austin.

Articles

Amsden, Charles. "The Navajo Exile at Bosque Redondo." *New Mexico Historical Review* 8 (January, 1933) : 31–50.

Bloom, Lansing B. "The Reverand Hiram Walter Read, Baptist Missionary," *New Mexico Historical Review* 17 (April, 1942) : 113–147.

Cheetham, Francis T. "The First Term of the American Court in Taos, New Mexico." *New Mexico Historical Review* 1 (January, 1926) : 23–41.

Dawson, Thomas F. "Major Thompson, Chief Ouray and the Utes." *Colorado Magazine* 7 (May, 1930) : 113–122.

Ellis, Richard N., ed. "Bent, Carson, and the Indians, 1865." *Colorado Magazine* 46 (Winter, 1969) : 55–68.

Foster, James M., Jr. "Fort Bascom, New Mexico." *New Mexico Historical Review* 35 (January, 1960) : 30–62.

Gressley, Gene M., ed. "Report on Ft. Garland Made by Christopher (Kit) Carson to Major Roger James, June 10, 1866." *Colorado Magazine* 32 (July, 1955) : 215–224.

Jenkins, Myra Ellen. "Taos Pueblo and Its Neighbors, 1540–1847." *New Mexico Historical Review* 41 (April, 1966) : 85–114.

Martin, Cornelia Williams. "Sketch of the Life of Governor Throop." *Cayuga County Historical Society Collections* 7 (1889) : 155–167.

McNitt, Frank. "Old Fort Wingate." *El Palacio* 78 (1972) : 30–36.

Moody, Marshall D. "Kit Carson, Agent to the Indians in New Mexico, 1853–1861." *New Mexico Historical Review* 28 (January, 1953) : 1–20.

Morrison, William B. "Fort Arbuckle." *Chronicles of Oklahoma* 6 (March, 1928) : 26–34.

Murphy, Lawrence R. "Rayado: Pioneer Settlement in Northeastern New Mexico, 1848–1857." *New Mexico Historical Review* 46 (January, 1971) : 37–56.

Myres, Sandra L. "Evy Alexander: The Colonel's Lady at McDowell in Arizona." *Montana: The Magazine of Western History* 24 (Summer, 1974) : 26–38.

Nankivell, John H. "Fort Garland, Colorado." *Colorado Magazine* 16 (January, 1939) : 13–27.

Read, Benjamin H. "The Last Word on 'Montezuma.' " *New Mexico Historical Review* 1 (July, 1926) : 350–358.

Reeve, Frank D. "The Federal Indian Policy in New Mexico, 1858–1880." *New Mexico Historical Review* 12 (July, 1937): 218–269; and 13 (January, 1938): 14–62; (April, 1938): 146–191; (July, 1938): 261–313.

Russell, Mrs. Hal. "Memoirs of Marian Russell." *Colorado Magazine* 20 (July, 1943): 140–153; (September, 1943): 181–195; (November, 1943): 226–237; and 21 (January, 1944): 29–37; (March, 1944): 62–73; (May, 1944): 101–111.

Shirk, George H., ed. "The Lost Colonel." *Chronicles of Oklahoma* 35 (Summer, 1957) : 180–193.

Taylor, Morris F. "Ka-ni-ache." *Colorado Magazine* 43 (Fall, 1966): 275–302; and 44 (Spring, 1967) : 139–161.

Thompson, Albert W. "Kit Carson's Camp Nichols in No Man's Land." *Colorado Magazine* 11 (September, 1934) : 179–185.

Utley, Robert M. "Arizona Vanquished." *The American West* 6 (November, 1969) : 16–22.

———. "Fort Union and the Santa Fe Trail." *New Mexico Historical Review* 36 (January, 1961) : 36–48.

Wright, Muriel. "A History of Fort Cobb." *Chronicles of Oklahoma* 34 (Spring, 1956) : 53–71.

Books

Adams, Eleanor B., and Angélico Chávez, trans. and eds. *The Missions of New Mexico, 1776: A Description by Fray Francisco Atanasio Dominquez with Other Contemporary Documents*. Albuquerque: University of New Mexico Press, 1956.

Ambrose, Stephen E. *Upton and the Army*. Baton Rouge: Louisiana State University Press, 1964.

Athearn, Robert G. *William Tecumseh Sherman and the Settlement of the West*. Norman: University of Oklahoma Press, 1956.

Bailey, Lynn R. *Bosque Redondo: An American Concentration Camp*. Pasadena, Calif.: Socio-Technical Books, 1970.

———. *The Long Walk: A History of the Navajo Wars, 1846–68*. Los Angeles: Westernlore Press, 1964.

Bandelier, Adolph F., and Edgar L. Hewett. *Indians of the Rio Grande Valley*. Albuquerque: University of New Mexico Press, 1937.

Bannon, John Francis. *The Spanish Borderlands Frontier, 1513–1821.* New York: Holt, Rinehart, Winston, 1970.

Bearss, Edwin C., and Arrell M. Gibson. *Fort Smith: Little Gibraltar on the Arkansas.* Norman: University of Oklahoma Press, 1969.

Beck, Warren A. *New Mexico: A History of Four Centuries.* Norman: University of Oklahoma Press, 1962.

Biddle, Ellen McGowen. *Reminiscences of a Soldier's Wife.* Philadelphia: J. B. Lippincott, 1907.

Bonsal, Stephen. *Edward Fitzgerald Beale: A Pioneer in the Path of Empire, 1822–1903.* New York and London: G. P. Putnam's Sons, 1912.

Bourke, Captain John G. *On the Border with Crook.* Chicago: Rio Grande Press, 1962.

Bunting, Bainbridge. *Taos Adobes: Spanish Colonial and Territorial Architecture of the Taos Valley.* Santa Fe: Museum of New Mexico Press, 1964.

Carter, Harvey Lewis. *'Dear Old Kit': The Historical Christopher Carson.* Norman: University of Oklahoma Press, 1968.

Carter, Captain Robert G. *On the Border with Mackenzie: Or Winning West Texas from the Comanches.* New York: Antiquarian Press, 1961.

Colton, Ray Charles. *The Civil War in the Western Territories: Arizona, Colorado, New Mexico, and Utah.* Norman: University of Oklahoma Press, 1959.

Crocchiola, F. L. [F. Stanley]. *The Civil War in New Mexico.* Denver: World Press, 1960.

———. *Fort Bascom: Comanche-Kiowa Barrier.* Pampa, Tex.: privately published, 1961.

———. *Fort Craig.* Pampa, Tex.: privately published, 1963.

———. *Fort Union.* Canadian, Tex.: privately published, 1953.

Crook, George. *General George Crook: His Autobiography.* Ed. Martin F. Schmitt. Norman: University of Oklahoma Press, 1946.

Custer, Elizabeth B. *"Boots and Saddles"; Or, Life in Dakota with General Custer.* Norman: University of Oklahoma Press, 1961.

———. *Following the Guidon.* Norman: University of Oklahoma Press, 1966.

———. *Tenting on the Plains: Or, General Custer in Kansas and Texas.* 3 vols. Norman: University of Oklahoma Press, 1971.

Debo, Angie. *The Rise and Fall of the Choctaw Republic.* Norman: University of Oklahoma Press, 1934.

Deibert, Ralph C. *A History of the Third United States Cavalry.* Harrisburg, Pa.: Telegraph Press, 1933.

Dobyns, Henry F., and R. C. Euler. *The Ghost Dance of 1889 among the Indians of Northwestern Arizona.* Prescott, Ariz.: Prescott College Press, 1967.

Drumm, Stella M., ed. *Down the Santa Fe Trail and into New Mexico: The Diary of Susan Shelby Magoffin, 1846–1847.* New Haven: Yale University Press, 1926.

Emmett, Chris. *Fort Union and the Winning of the Southwest.* Norman: University of Oklahoma Press, 1965.

Estergreen, M. Morgan. *Kit Carson: A Portrait in Courage.* Norman: University of Oklahoma Press, 1962.

Favour, Alpheus H. *Old Bill Williams, Mountain Man.* Norman: University of Oklahoma Press, 1962.

Federal Writers' Project. *Arkansas: A Guide to the State.* New York: Hastings House, 1941.

———. *Colorado: A Guide to the Highest State.* New York: Hastings House, 1941.

———. *Illinois: A Descriptive and Historical Guide.* Chicago: A. C. McClurg & Co., 1939.

———. *New Mexico: A Guide to the Colorful State.* New York: Hastings House, 1940.

———. *Oklahoma: A Guide to the Sooner State.* Norman: University of Oklahoma Press, 1941.

Foreman, Grant, ed. *A Pathfinder in the Southwest: The Itinerary of Lieutenant A. W. Whipple.* Norman: University of Oklahoma Press, 1941.

Frazer, Robert W. *Forts of the West: Military Forts and Presidios and Posts Commonly Called Forts West of the Mississippi River to 1898.* Norman: University of Oklahoma Press, 1965.

Garrard, Lewis H. *Wah-To-Yah and the Taos Trail.* Norman: University of Oklahoma Press, 1955.

Goetzmann, William H. *Army Exploration in the American West, 1803–1863.* New Haven: Yale University Press, 1959.

Grant, Blanche C. *When Old Trails Were New: The Story of Taos.* New York: Press of the Pioneers, 1934.

Hafen, LeRoy R., ed. *The Mountain Men and the Fur Trade of the Far West.* 9 vols. Glendale, Calif.: Arthur H. Clark, 1965–1968.

———, and Ann W. Hafen, eds. *Frémont's Fourth Expedition: A Documentary Account of the Disaster, 1848–49.* Glendale, Calif.: Arthur H. Clark, 1960.

Jackson, W. Turrentine. *Wagon Roads West: A Study of Federal Road Surveys and Construction in the Trans-Mississippi West, 1846–1869.* New Haven: Yale University Press, 1964.

Keleher, William A. *Maxwell Land Grant: A New Mexico Item.* Santa Fe: The Rydal Press, 1942.

———. *Turmoil in New Mexico, 1846–1868.* Santa Fe: The Rydal Press, 1952.

Kelly, Lawrence C. *Navajo Roundup: Selected Correspondence of Kit Carson's Expedition against the Navajo, 1863–1865.* Boulder, Colo.: Pruett Publishing Co., 1970.

Kidder, Alfred Vincent. *An Introduction to the Study of Southwestern Archaeology with a Preliminary Account of the Excavations at Pecos.* New Haven: Yale University Press, 1962.

Kluckhohn, Clyde, and Dorothy Leighton. *The Navajo.* Cambridge: Harvard University Press, 1946.

Kubler, George. *The Religious Architecture of New Mexico in the Colonial*

Period and Since the American Occupation. Colorado Springs: The Taylor Museum, 1940.

La Farge, Oliver (with Arthur N. Morgan). *Santa Fe: The Autobiography of a Southwestern Town.* Norman: University of Oklahoma Press, 1959.

Lamar, Howard R. *The Far Southwest, 1846–1912: A Territorial History.* New Haven: Yale University Press, 1966.

Lange, Charles H., and Carroll L. Riley, eds. *The Southwestern Journals of Adolph F. Bandelier, 1880–1882.* Albuquerque: University of New Mexico Press, 1966.

Lane, Lydia Spencer. *I Married a Soldier; Or, Old Days in the Army.* Albuquerque: Horn & Wallace, 1964.

Leckie, William H. *The Buffalo Soldiers: A Narrative of the Negro Cavalry in the West.* Norman: University of Oklahoma Press, 1967.

Linton, Ralph, ed. *Acculturation in Seven American Indian Tribes.* New York: D. Appleton–Century Co., 1940.

Lowe, Percival G. *Five Years a Dragoon ('49 to '54): And Other Adventures on the Great Plains.* Ed. Don Russell. Norman: University of Oklahoma Press, 1965.

Luce, Edward S. *Keogh, Comanche and Custer.* Saint Louis: John S. Swift Co., 1939.

Martin, Cornelia Williams. *The Old Home.* 2 vols. Auburn, N.Y.: privately published, 1894.

Martin, Edward S. *Some Account of Family Stocks Involved in Life at Willowbrook.* New York: privately published, 1933.

Meline, James F. *Two Thousand Miles on Horseback: Santa Fe and Back, a Summer Tour through Kansas, Nebraska, Colorado and New Mexico in the Year 1866.* Albuquerque: Horn & Wallace, 1966.

Möllhausen, H. Balduin. *Diary of a Journey from the Mississippi to the Coasts of the Pacific with a United States Government Expedition.* 2 vols. London: Longman, Brown, 1858.

Murphy, Lawrence R. *Philmont: A History of New Mexico's Cimarron County.* Albuquerque: University of New Mexico Press, 1972.

Nevins, Allan. *Frémont, Pathmarker of the West.* New York: D. Appleton–Century Co., 1939.

Nye, Wilbur S. *Carbine and Lance: The Story of Old Fort Sill.* Norman: University of Oklahoma Press, 1937.

———. *Plains Indian Raiders: The Final Phases of Warfare from the Arkansas to the Red River.* Norman: University of Oklahoma Press, 1968.

Parsons, Elsie C. *Pueblo Indian Religion.* 2 vols. Chicago: University of Chicago Press, 1939.

Pearson, Jim Berry. *The Maxwell Land Grant.* Norman: University of Oklahoma Press, 1961.

Peters, DeWitt C. *The Life and Adventures of Kit Carson.* New York: W. R. C. Clark & Co., 1858.

Prucha, Francis Paul. *A Guide to the Military Posts of the United States, 1789–1895.* Madison: State Historical Society of Wisconsin, 1964.

Riddle, Kenyon. *Records and Maps of the Old Santa Fe Trail*. West Palm Beach, Fla.: privately published, 1963.

Rockwell, Wilson. *The Utes, a Forgotten People*. Denver: Sage Books, 1956.

Rusling, James F. *Across America; Or, the Great West and the Pacific Coast*. New York: Sheldon & Co., 1874.

Sabin, Edwin L. *Kit Carson Days (1809–1868)*. Chicago: A. C. McClurg & Co., 1914.

———. *Kit Carson Days, 1809–1868: Adventures in the Path of Empire*. 2 vols. New York: Press of the Pioneers, 1935.

Sheridan, Philip H. *Personal Memoirs of P. H. Sheridan*. 2 vols. New York: D. Appleton & Co., 1888.

Sherman, William Tecumseh. *Memoirs of General William T. Sherman*. 2 vols. New York: C. L. Webster & Co., 1891.

Shinkle, James D. *Fort Sumner and the Bosque Redondo Indian Reservation*. Roswell, N.M.: Hall-Poorbaugh Press, 1965.

Smith, William Ernest. *The Francis Preston Blair Family in Politics*. 2 vols. New York: Macmillan Co., 1933.

Sonnichsen, C. L. *The Mescalero Apaches*. Norman: University of Oklahoma Press, 1958.

Spicer, Edward H. *Cycles of Conquest: The Impact of Spain, Mexico and the United States on the Indians of the Southwest, 1533–1960*. Tucson: University of Arizona Press, 1962.

Summerhayes, Martha. *Vanished Arizona: Recollections of the Army Life of a New England Woman*. Glorieta, N.M.: Rio Grande Press, 1970.

Sweeny, Thomas W. *Journal of Lt. Thomas W. Sweeny, 1849–1853*. Ed. Arthur Woodward. Los Angeles: Westernlore Press, 1956.

Twitchell, Ralph E. *The Leading Facts of New Mexican History*. 2 vols. Albuquerque: Horn & Wallace, 1963.

———. *Old Santa Fe: The Story of New Mexico's Ancient Capital*. Santa Fe: New Mexican Publishing Corp., 1925.

Underhill, Ruth M. *The Navajos*. Norman: University of Oklahoma Press, 1956.

Utley, Robert M. *Fort Union National Monument, New Mexico*. Washington, D.C.: United States Department of the Interior, National Park Service, 1962.

Vielé, Teresa. *"Following the Drum": A Glimpse of Frontier Life*. Ed. James M. Day. Austin: Steck Vaughn, 1968.

Wallace, Ernest, and E. Adamson Hoebel. *The Comanches: Lords of the South Plains*. Norman: University of Oklahoma, 1952.

Weber, David J. *The Taos Trappers: The Fur Trade in the Far Southwest, 1540–1846*. Norman: University of Oklahoma Press, 1971.

Whitman, Sidney E. *The Troopers: An Informal History of the Plains Cavalry, 1865–1890*. New York: Hastings House, 1962.

Wilson, James B. *The Life and Services of Brevet Brigadier General Andrew Jonathan Alexander*. New York: privately published, 1887.

Wright, Muriel H. *A Guide to the Indian Tribes of Oklahoma*. Norman: University of Oklahoma Press, 1951.

Bibliography

Reference Works and Biographical Dictionaries

Dictionary of American Biography. 12 vols. New York: Charles Scribner's Sons, 1964.

Dyer, Frederick H. *A Compendium of the War of the Rebellion.* 3 vols. New York: T. Yoseloff, 1959.

Heitman, Francis B. *Historical Register and Dictionary of the United States Army from Its Organization, September 29, 1789, to March 2, 1903.* 2 vols. Washington, D.C.: Government Printing Office, 1903.

Hodge, Frederick W., ed. *Handbook of American Indians North of Mexico.* 2 vols. Washington, D.C.: Government Printing Office, 1912.

Pearce, Thomas M., ed. *New Mexico Place Names: A Geographical Dictionary.* Albuquerque: University of New Mexico Press, 1965.

Webb, Walter P., and H. Bailey Carroll, eds. *Handbook of Texas.* 2 vols. Austin: Texas State Historical Association, 1952.

Wheat, Carl I. *Mapping the Transmississippi West, 1540–1861.* 5 vols. San Francisco: The Institute of Historical Cartography, 1960.

Who Was Who in America, 1897–1942. Chicago: Marquis Publications, 1942.

Newspapers

Auburn, N.Y., *Morning News.* October 26, 1877.

Denver *Daily Rocky Mountain News.* October 11, 1866.
    October 27, 1866.

Santa Fe *New Mexican.* November 3, 1866.
    December 1, 1866.

Santa Fe *Weekly Gazette.* September 8, 1866.
    September 29, 1866.

Index